I0820025

Selected Essays
of Ludvig Holberg

Selected Essays of Ludvig Holberg

Translated from the *Epistler*

with an Introduction and Notes

by P. M. Mitchell

GREENWOOD PRESS, PUBLISHERS
WESTPORT, CONNECTICUT

Library of Congress Cataloging in Publication Data

Holberg, Ludvig, Baron, 1684-1754.
Selected essays of Ludvig Holberg.

Reprint of the 1955 ed. published by University of Kansas Press, Lawrence.
Includes bibliographical references and index.
[PT8086.5.E5M5 1976] 839.8'1'44 76-16842
ISBN 0-8371-8970-5

Originally published in 1955 by University of Kansas Press, Lawrence

Reprinted with the permission of The University Press of Kansas

Reprinted in 1976 by Greenwood Press,
a division of Williamhouse-Regency Inc.

Library of Congress Catalog Card Number 76-16842

ISBN 0-8371-8970-5

Printed in the United States of America

Preface

THE FIVE VOLUMES of Ludvig Holberg's *Epistler* were originally published in Copenhagen from 1748 to 1754. The first two volumes, comprising essays 1-183, appeared in 1748; the third and fourth volumes, containing essays 184-446, were added, 1749-50; the fifth volume, containing essays 447-539, appeared posthumously in 1754. An annotated edition of the *Epistler* was published by Christian Bruun, 1865-75. It has now been superseded by F. J. Billeskov Jansen's critical edition, begun in 1944 and completed in 1954.

Although Holberg is the greatest figure in the history of eighteenth century Scandinavian literature and although his essays are an important source of Scandinavian cultural history, the *Epistler* have remained inaccessible and unknown to the English-speaking world. I have here tried to select representative essays for translation, but at the same time I have favored essays of special interest to students of English history and literature.

As far as possible, I have based my work on the edition of Professor Billeskov Jansen, who has given invaluable help in preparing the commentary. Notes which have been furnished by him are identified by the symbol "BJ."

The descriptive titles of the essays are not by Holberg, who gave them numbers only.

I record with gratitude the financial assistance given me by Det danske Selskab, Copenhagen; the American-Scandinavian Foundation, New York; and the University of Kansas Endowment Association, Lawrence.

P. M. MITCHELL

Contents

INTRODUCTION

Ludvig Holberg's name has been preserved in world literature almost solely because he was a writer of comedy. His plays do represent his most effective medium. Like Plautus and Molière, whom he most closely resembles as a playwright, he is justly considered to be one of the great European writers of comedy. Holberg wrote comedies for the sake of comedy, just as he wrote histories for the sake of history, but in his comedies, histories, and many other works, he took considerable pride in adjudging himself a didactic moralist. Whether he wrote as an historian or as a satirist, whether he wrote plays or essays, he wished to be looked upon as a writer who could instill into his fellow men, and above all his countrymen, tolerance, better taste, common sense, and factual knowledge. Actually, he was an articulate rationalist, a cultural interpreter, a cyclopaedic compiler, a born author, and a wit. The moralizing attitude was prescribed by the times. In short, Holberg is a true representative of the first half of the eighteenth century, the Age of Enlightenment.

The ideas, the moral quality, and the didacticism which underlie Holberg's works, and especially the satires and the utopian imaginary voyage entitled *Niels Klim,* find more direct expression in his essays, *Moralske Tanker* ("Moral Thoughts," 1744) and the five volumes of his *Epistler* ("Epistles," 1748-54). It was not until Holberg adopted the form of the moral essay, that he had a free hand to develop his philosophy and his personal opinions unsystematically, and to express himself on any subject without feeling the restrictions of a literary form or the pervading discipline of a chosen historical subject.

In the essays and especially in the *Epistler,* Holberg speaks from the world of his experience and his reading. He writes as a man of the world, a philosopher, a dramatist, a critic, and an academician. He writes from the European world of learning which was peculiar to the seventeenth and eighteenth centuries, and as one of the learned who, so to speak, had been everywhere, seen everything, and read whatever was worth while. In the course of his long career as an author, he treated almost every subject with which a cultivated man might have concerned himself during the first half of the eighteenth century.

Geographically considered, Holberg had been born on the periphery of cultured Europe; but temporally considered, he had been born in an age of the secularization of culture. The Reformation had come to mean the nationalization of the church and the independent interpretation of religious matters. The way had been opened for the free discussion and interpretation of historical phenomena. In the seventeenth century there had developed a historiography outside the pale of the church, and a law which was divorced from the church, as well as a new emphasis on the idea of natural law. Philosophers delineated hitherto unimagined relationships in the world; these relationships in turn revealed what seemed to be a vast system of man's physical and moral existence that but awaited classification through the application of human reason and through scientific experimentation. At the time Holberg was born in distant Bergen, Norway, in 1684, the great minds of Europe were busy creating a cosmos out of chaos. Their thought was basically teleological; they assumed a divine pattern and therefore a divine purpose.

The political picture at the beginning of the eighteenth century was in marked contrast to the new intellectual freedom and to the coming religious liberalism, for the Age of Rationalism was also an age of absolutism. Louis XIV was the model for all Europe, and for the world of elegance and sophistication Versailles was the center of culture and politics. Denmark was still an important power at the beginning of the eighteenth century, politically speaking, but its culture, like that of the rest of Scandinavia, was largely derivative. Even the furniture and dress of the upper classes were in the French style. France, England, the Netherlands, and to a lesser extent politically disorganized Germany, were the centers of culture. To them Denmark's relation was that of a not too far removed planet; and if Denmark was a planet, then Norway was Denmark's moon. Compared with French literature, Danish literature scarcely existed. Generically, its significance did not extend beyond the folk song and the hymn. The language of the court was German, the polite language was French, and the academic language was Latin. The University of Copenhagen upheld the scholastic tradition; there were only two examinations to be taken, the philosophical and the theological. At an early age Holberg nevertheless determined upon an academic career. He finished his schooling in 1702 and set off for the University of Copenhagen, the only university in Denmark-Norway. Here he stayed until 1704. Even before he left Bergen, the most cosmopolitan spot in Norway, Holberg was not an unaccomplished linguist. His pursuit of languages during adolescence, his desire to study, and his will to travel all reflect the ambition, intellectual curiosity, and native intelligence with which he was endowed.

It is difficult for us to picture the Copenhagen to which Holberg came in 1702. While the city was the cultural center of Denmark-Norway, it was unlike the enlightened capitals of the major European states, and for an inquisitive and ambitious young Scandinavian, intellectual salvation lay in a journey to the fonts of European culture.

In 1704 Holberg began the first of his several voyages abroad. This trip, to the Netherlands and back, in no way resembled the grand tour of the contemporary young gentleman, for Holberg had very little money and had to live as simply as possible. He set out imbued with serious interest, wishing to gain an acquaintance with the centers of contemporary European culture, but lacking an entree to the studies of the great men whose works interested him. Subsequently Holberg made little mention of the journey to the Netherlands in 1704-5, but the Netherlands continued to exert an attraction for him. He again spent time there during two later sojourns abroad, 1714-16 and 1725-26.

The choice of the Netherlands as the first country to be visited was not accidental. In the late seventeenth century, the Netherlands had become the intellectual heart of Europe. It was a haven for oppressed thinkers, sectarians, and dissenters. It was a central point for the exchange of ideas and news of a theological, philosophical, political, and literary nature. Here exiles and refugees found comparative freedom of speech and of the press. Here was neutral territory for religious factions. Consequently, the Netherlands had become the center for the popularization of knowledge, the great European book market of the day, and, as has been said, the clearing house of European thought. French was the idiom of the refugees who assembled there, and new ideas spread from the Low Countries through the easy medium of the French language. Here was Jean Le Clerc, the Swiss-born editor of several encyclopaedic periodicals and a friend of Locke and Shaftesbury. Here lived Pierre Bayle, Holberg's favorite author, an exile from France and the compiler of the *Dictionaire historique et critique* (first edition, 1697), a publication which later was to mean more to Holberg than any other single work. Bayle's dictionary, a sort of biographical and geographical cyclopaedia, is the first monument of the French encyclopaedists. Holberg discusses it in Epistle 34. Bayle's repeated statement, which at that time was the ultimate in the secularization of culture and in tolerance, that it was conceivable for a society of atheists to live in harmony, had called down the wrath of many believers, and Bayle's ideas were the direct motivation for Leibniz in writing the *Théodicée*.

With England, where he lived from 1706 to 1708, Holberg was well pleased. Queen Anne's reign, that "age of prose," was a period of greater personal freedom under a more representative government than Holberg had experienced before. In his *Anhang . . .* , published in 1713, Holberg called England "the Northern Paradise" and the English "a free people." English belles-lettres had perhaps declined at the end of the seventeenth century, when French critics came to be accepted as authoritative, but a new contemporary literature was arising out of the pervading spirit of rationalism, and as a result of the popular concern with religious and moral questions. Holberg's English contemporaries–Swift, Addison, Steele, Defoe–were in these and the next few years to shape a new and great English prose literature. Holberg was exposed to the same currents of the time as they, breathed the same air as they, and consequently brought home to Denmark a general understanding of England which was to bear much fruit. Yet the significance of Holberg's stay in England, or more specifically at Oxford, is difficult to ascertain and has been the subject of inconclusive learned discussion. In his autobiography, Holberg treats his stay at Oxford anecdotally and gives few clues to his knowledge of contemporary English letters. Although he lived and studied in Oxford, Holberg never matriculated at the university. He states that his first work, the scholarly *Introduction til de fornemste Europæiske Rigers Historier* ("Introduction to the History of the Leading European Powers," 1711) after the manner of Pufendorf, was conceived in the Bodleian Library.

It is erroneous to assume that Holberg's choice of England as a place for study was unique or very unusual. In his biography of the young Holberg, Th. A. Müller pointed out that no less than seventy-two Scandinavians, the majority from Denmark, studied at Oxford during the years 1682-1708. Several of the professors at the University of Copenhagen had spent some time in England. To a certain extent, therefore, Holberg was following a tradition in going to England.

In 1708-09, Holberg had occasion to spend several months in Germany, but his experiences there seem to have meant comparatively little to him, and nowhere aroused in him the same enthusiasm as when he dealt with the culture of France, England, and the Netherlands. This was perhaps because the Germans dared no more than the Danes to be themselves. One could not even perceive in embryo the Athenian age of Weimar or what within a century was to become the all-conquering German philosophy.

Upon his return to Copenhagen in 1709, Holberg became the prototype of the ambitious young academician who would wrest recognition from university and civil authorities by his scholarly production. He aspired to a chair at the university. His goal was not easy, for the number of professorships was small, and each professor was expected to be a polymath. According to the prevailing system, a member of the faculty advanced in rank by progressing from one professorship to another. The lowest professorship, in metaphysics, was held by the most recently appointed professor.

From 1709 to 1714, Holberg enjoyed a collegiate stipend which enabled him to devote most of his time to scholarly pursuits. During these years he published his first work, the *Introduction* . . . in 1711 (and its supplement, the *Anhang* . . . , in 1713) and prepared his *Introduction til Natur- og Folke-Rettens Kundskab* (published in 1716). This early scholarly production gave evidence of the New Learning, as opposed to medieval scholasticism, but it was the New Learning of the seventeenth century, of Grotius and Pufendorf, and not yet of the eighteenth century. Nevertheless, Holberg's works were radical enough in themselves, for they were written not in Latin or even in French, but in Danish. This fact gives them their lasting significance. Although Holberg was often to employ Latin, he now and later wrote Danish as a matter of principle; he wanted to write not only for the academic world or the elegant world, but also for his fellow-countrymen. He saw no reason why the language of the people could not be employed for the communication and dissemination of knowledge.

In 1714 Holberg was named *professor designatus*—that is, he was promised the first vacancy on the faculty of the University of Copenhagen. Heartened by the security of this promise, he hastened abroad in order to fulfill the provisions of the stipend which he held. This journey, via the Netherlands to France and Italy, was his most adventurous. Holberg was now more mature and more open to the intellectual currents of the time, but he was scarcely better off financially. His stipend was small, and the new professorial dignity carried with it no remuneration. A detailed and witty account of the remarkable journey which took him to Paris and then to Rome and then—on foot—back to Paris again, can be read in Holberg's autobiography. Paris was the central point of his sojourn abroad, for, with respect to learning, "France was its chosen seat, and there was no country in the world where a greater proficiency might be made, or a better taste formed, in all the liberal arts," as Holberg later wrote in his autobiography. Holberg felt a great personal debt to France. "I confess," he continues, "that I owe everything to French books . . . ." Holberg's stay in Paris has given rise to hypotheses about the French origins of Holberg's comedies and about his indebtedness to contemporary French literature. To be sure, Holberg entered the world of rococo French literature, of the *Mercure galant,* and of Boileau when he came to Paris, but prior to the year 1716 there is no evidence of any penetrating belletristic interest on his part. Holberg was a wandering scholar and not yet a man of letters.

In Paris Holberg visited libraries assiduously and evinced great interest in religious questions. In Catholic France he suddenly became a defender of the Protestant faith. Like so many of his beliefs and opinions, Holberg's Protestantism was a reaction; until he was confronted with aggressive and proselytizing Catholicism, he was little concerned with ecclesiastical differences.

For Holberg, as for his time, Italy was to a considerable extent overshadowed by France. Italy was post-classical, baroque Italy; it was not yet the temple of art and the classical ideal which grew out of Winckelmann's enthusiastic appreciation. Albeit the center of the Christian world and a seat of learning, it was still looked upon as an antiquarian curiosity. This was the attitude of the times, and it was Holberg's attitude. Holberg's reactions to what he experienced and his evaluations of what he saw in his travels were usually typical of the times, and typical of the tourist—in the tradition of the Grand Tour—in the Age of Enlightenment.

Holberg returned to Copenhagen in 1717 and the following year he finally became Professor of Metaphysics, "although against my inclination," as he lamented. He termed this appointment "thralldom for two years," and remarked that metaphysics never had been in greater danger than when he professed it. His release came two years later, when he became Professor of Latin Literature and Secretary of the University.

While Professor of Metaphysics, the enterprising young scholar turned to a kind of intellectual activity for which he seemed totally unprepared. He began to write satires. The occasion seems to have been a learned dispute with a colleague whom he satirized in Latin in 1719. In any case, Holberg soon discovered his talent and undertook to write satires for their own sake, after the fashion of Juvenal and Boileau. In so doing, he became a popular writer and started a chain of events which soon led to the production of some of the great comedies in world literature.

Under the pseudonym of Hans Mickelsen, Holberg published in 1719-20 a mock-heroic poem entitled *Peder Paars,* which parodied classical heroic poetry, particularly Virgil's. For these as for his other satires, Holberg names Boileau, Montaigne, and Juvenal as his models. *Peder Paars* was a sensation on the Danish book market and became the "best seller" of the day. For the first time there had been produced in Denmark a Danish work of belles-lettres which was widely circulated, which became popular literature, and which was read at the several levels of Danish society. Although not a great work of literature, *Peder Paars,* which is a satire on the ignorance of the gullible, has some attributes of a classic.

In 1722 the former director of the court theater, a Frenchman, obtained consent from the crown to establish a theater in the Danish capital. This theater was to have the peculiar function of presenting comedies in Danish—but there were no Danish comedies. Comedies had therefore either to be translated from the French or written in Danish expressly for the new theater. Necessity became the mother of dramatic invention. Holberg was now Professor of Latin Literature at the university and in his thirty-sixth year. He was also the author of *Peder Paars* and consequently the most widely read Danish writer—a man who, despite his rather solitary life and academic interests, obviously had a sense of humor. Holberg was approached by persons interested in the new theatrical venture. Convinced by arguments of which we know nothing, he agreed to write a series of comedies for the Danish theater. There are few parallels to the literary production which now followed. Without preparation and apparently without hitherto having paid particular attention to the drama, Holberg wrote no less than twenty-seven plays in two years. Although quickly written, the plays are cleverly constructed and are good comedy. As a dramatist, Holberg was at all times aware of his literary indebtedness to Plautus and Molière, whom he accepted as models and whose praises he never ceased to sing. The *Epistler* contain many laudatory references to both older dramatists. Holberg has implied that there were only three great writers of comedy: Plautus, Molière, and—Holberg. "One can say that in the 2,000 years between Plautus and Molière no decent comedy saw the light of day," wrote Holberg in Epistle 190; and for the post-Molière comedy in France he had only contempt. Just as Molière had reworked classical Roman, Spanish, and Italian comedies and made each of his comedies into an original work, Holberg likewise adapted, localized, and recast extant dramatic raw material and knew how to make the best use of his predecessors. Although he used Plautus as a model thrice, and was inspired by the plays and dramatic devices of Molière, he did not rewrite or plagiarize from either author. Holberg's finished product contained no alien elements; it was adapted to the local scene and the characters were luminously comprehensible to the Danish bourgeoisie.

Holberg probably never really knew how good a playwright he was, for he was always anxious to make sure that a prospective critic was aware that the plays were morally didactic comedies of character and, as he said, capable of amusing and instructing at the same time. Reflecting on his plays as a sexagenarian, Holberg wrote apologetically that he thought them "not unworthy of a philosopher and an old man." Although the comedies were well received in the theater in Lille Grönnegade in Copenhagen and won there the applause of hearers of "unspoiled taste," which according to Holberg was the test of good comedy, he was unquestionably tantalized by a desire to win acclaim from Molière's countrymen, and above all from French comedians. The "natural good taste" of the Danish bourgeoisie could never give such satisfaction as a nod of recognition that might come from Paris or perhaps Amsterdam. One wonders whether there is not some bitterness in Holberg's scolding at the "corrupt taste of the Parisians" and at the root of his opinion that the French are overcritical of foreigners writing in their language.

Holberg stopped writing comedies almost as suddenly as he had begun. Perhaps he was tired of writing them. He called his playwriting "difficult and costly work" which brought little more than trouble and envy to his door. Whether he enjoyed any remuneration for his comedies is impossible to establish. Holberg was hypochondriac and penurious; he continually implied that he profited little from the sale of his books. But all evidence speaks against him. He was his own publisher, and he died a wealthy man. In order to deprive middlemen of profiting from the sale of his books, he not only published but also sold them himself. With a few exceptions his books sold well.

The journey abroad in 1725-26—Holberg's last—was more staid than the earlier travels. As a matter of fact, it was nominally undertaken for the sake of his health. Although his fame had yet to spread beyond the boundaries of the Danish-Norwegian kingdom, he was now a member of the fraternity of learned men, and he visited several of the scholars whom he previously had admired at a distance. While in Amsterdam, on his way back to Denmark, he called upon Jean Le Clerc. This was probably the most invigorating acquaintance Holberg made, for he had great respect and admiration for Le Clerc. While in Paris he visited numerous libraries, but his autobiography, as usual, gives few hints as to the way he really spent his time or as to what he read.

Holberg returned to a Copenhagen that was coming more and more under the influence of pietism. Count Zinsendorf had won great influence at the Danish court a dozen years before and although the life of the monarch, Frederik IV, was far from exemplary, evidences of worldliness among the population of the Danish capital were frowned on. In 1727, the theater was temporarily closed, and three years later it was closed permanently. A new theater was not established until more than twenty years later. In the intervening years several editions of the comedies were printed, but Holberg had no reason to concern himself with the drama again until 1750, when, at the age of sixty-five, he wrote seven new comedies for the theater which he had helped to re-establish.

After the closing of the theater, Holberg's scholarly production increased. He had become Professor of History in 1730—one might say "at last," for history was his chosen field of interest. The quantity of Holberg's historical and topographical works is quite as imposing as that of his comedies. From 1729 through 1743 he published a description of Denmark and Norway (mentioned above), a history of Denmark in three volumes, a synopsis of universal history (in Latin), a description of Bergen, a general church history, a history of the Jews in two volumes, and two volumes containing the biographies of great men after the manner of Plutarch. During the same years he found time to re-edit his comedies, to write in Latin the imaginary voyage *Niels Klim,* to compose 900 Latin epigrams, and to write parts two and three of his autobiography (in Latin), as well as several lesser works.

Of his historical works, the history of Denmark (*Dannemarks Riges Historie,* I-III, 1732-35), is of primary importance. The earlier *Introduction* was the first universal (i.e., European) history written in Danish and the first modern historical work directed at the general reading public; the history of Denmark was similarly the first history of Denmark readily accessible to the public.

Nicolai Klimii iter subterraneum (1741)—"Niels Klim's Journey to the Underground"—was to the taste of the times and found a receptive European audience. Translations into German, Dutch, and French appeared during the year of publication, and translations into Danish and English the next year. A Swedish translation followed in 1746, and by the time Holberg died in 1754, a new German edition had been reprinted three times and a second French edition had been published. The idea of *Niels Klim* is very similar to that of *Gulliver's Travels:* a satirical imaginary voyage to a series of unknown lands where human vices and virtues are flayed or extolled by means of contrast, paradox, and exaggeration. Niels Klim visits a number of fantastic and exotic countries underground; they give Holberg an opportunity satirically to moralize on many subjects and to unleash acidly humorous criticism against superstition, religious controversy, academic disputation, ephemeral literature, and human folly in general and also to agitate for rational thinking, the emancipation of women, and other favorite ideas, to say nothing of his satirization of rhetorical devices such as the Homeric hyperbole.

Holberg's *Moralske Tanker* ("Moral Thoughts," 1744) was not inaccurately named "the Danish Spectator" by its Dutch translator in 1747. In adopting the essay genre, Holberg appealed to the taste of the time, but his was not the sophisticated wittiness of *The Spectator;* nor did he represent the urbane culture of men like Addison and Steele. The popularity of *Moralske Tanker* is attested by translations of the book into German, French, and Dutch. Whereas the *Epistler* were to be more cyclopaedic in nature, the "Moral Thoughts" comprised essays on matters of principle, social criticism, and metaphysical, religious, and philosophical questions. These essays lack the wit and sarcasm which Holberg felt freer to employ in his comedies and in the so-called Epistles. Each essay nominally expounds the Latin epigram which introduces it. He who would deduce Holberg's personal philosophy from his work should use *Moralske Tanker* as his primary source of information.

Introduction

Holberg was growing old. By the time the first volumes of *Epistler* were published in 1748, he was in his sixty-fourth year, but his intellectual vigor and his productive capacity were unabated. He was as prolific a writer as ever. His *Heltinde-Historier* ("Histories of Great Women") had appeared in 1745 and his translation of Herodian and an edition of his own lesser works in 1746. Holberg continued to write "Epistles," so that by 1753 he had written some 540 of them on a great variety of subjects. They filled five volumes and in all about 2,000 pages. In his last years he also published an oration on King Frederik IV (1746), a revised and augmented edition of his Latin epigrams (1749), a volume of prose fables (1751), as well as *Lettres . . . sur les mémoires concernant la reine Christine* (1752), and his own French translation of those of his Epistles which dealt with Montesquieu's *L'Esprit des loix* (1753). One is reminded of what Holberg wrote of Bayle's dictionary in Epistle 34: "This is a work which exceeds one man's powers."

Although the Epistles invoke the reader's experience, they are themselves the products of Holberg's study and of his intercourse with books. They contain the judgments and opinions of a man who has experienced much, but who now meditates and who receives his inspiration almost exclusively from the printed word. Holberg was an avid but not an indiscriminate reader. Because of his familiarity with cyclopaedic works and compendious reviews, he was probably as well informed about the European scene as any man in Denmark. At first glance, Holberg seems to have been acquainted with a fabulous number of books. An examination of his sources and use of quotations reveals that he was mainly dependent on a relatively small number of standard and periodical publications. In his remarkable disquisition *Holberg som Epigrammatiker og Essayist* (I-II, Copenhagen, 1938-39), and in his edition of the *Epistler*, F. J. Billeskov Jansen has conclusively demonstrated Holberg's dependence on certain works, and above all on Bayle's dictionary, Chambers' *Cyclopædia,* Le Gendre's *Traité historique et critique de l'Opinion,* the various *Bibliothèques* edited by Jean Le Clerc, and the *Bibliothèque Britannique.* Through painstaking study and clever analysis, Professor Billeskov Jansen has given much insight into Holberg's method of writing. Holberg would either read for inspiration in one of his favorite books or, having conceived an idea, refer to a likely heading in a cyclopaedic work. It therefore becomes relatively easy for us to retrace his steps in many cases and to establish his sources of information, his quotations and allusions. We are thus better able to understand Holberg and the working of his mind in the composition of various essays. Holberg's attitude was that, if a standard work contained an adequate treatment of the subject in hand, he might accept and rewrite part of it, making use of the source material, quotations, and opinions cited. In so doing he demonstrated himself to be a typical scholar of the eighteenth century. All this does not mean that Holberg did not read *in extenso.* That he did is evidenced by his histories as well as those essays treating matters not embraced by the cyclopaedic works. The tenth part of Holberg's own library, reconstructed by Christian Bruun in 1869, consisted of over 300 volumes.

Holberg read principally two sorts of literature. The first was the French literature published in the Netherlands. Despite Holberg's residence in England in his youth, he even seems in later years to have kept up his acquaintance with English literature through the intermediary of the Netherlands. He was to no little extent dependent on French abstracts of English books. This is but indicative of the fact that French, like Latin, was a medium of exchange in the learned and cultured world. Second in importance to French books was the Latin literature of classical Rome. Holberg's thinking rested squarely on the foundation of the Latin classics. The idea of a "classical education," vanishing in the twentieth century, was the only educational ideal of the eighteenth century. Holberg and his contemporaries accepted the ideas of Roman thinkers as modern ideas which stood in contrast to the metaphysical abstractions of the Middle Ages.

Introduction

If we put the question why Holberg wrote the *Epistler,* the answer would be roughly: he wrote in reaction to his reading and in order to propagate the idea of tolerance and moderation in all things. Time and again in the *Epistler,* Holberg states that his is the "middle path" or, in the case of a controversial matter, that "he takes no sides." Holberg's ideal was non-extremism; he was a severe critic of every sort of enthusiasm and fanaticism. His religion was moral, ethical, and intellectual, without a trace of emotional experience. Indeed, it is rather difficult to ascertain what Holberg's positive beliefs were. While his attitude often is negative, he is no destructive or nihilistic critic. Whether the subject of an individual essay is religious belief, scientific theory, or philosophy, the substance of the "Epistles" is an appeal to moderation and reason.

Holberg was not afraid of controversial issues. On the contrary, he felt that they generally could be resolved if the facts were laid bare and the principles of moderation and reason were applied. With certain great problems, as for example that of the co-existence of good and evil, he grappled repeatedly. Curiously enough, many of the "Epistles" lean toward the metaphysical, although Holberg was far from being a friend of abstractions or a mystic. From about 1743 on he was concerned with religious problems and the meaning of existence. This concern reflects only a tendency common to all thinking men; Holberg is the Everyman of a life well spent, who faces death without fear or remorse. His standpoint is ethical and moral rather than theological. Despite his discussion of fundamentally theological questions, Holberg was thoroughly secularized. He resembled not a little the English Deists and Naturalists, of whom he believed himself to be a severe critic.

It should be evident that Holberg's interests were not primarily belletristic. He was imbued with the universal spirit of the eighteenth century. His mind had as many facets as Bayle's dictionary or Chambers' cyclopaedia. The title-page of the *Epistler* typifies Holberg and his times; it promises "historical, political, metaphysical, moral, philosophical, and amusing" essays. Neither in a figurative nor in a literal sense was Holberg a professor bound to a single subject. He evinced interest not only in the many branches of human knowledge which affected his life, but, like his contemporaries, also in the exotic. On subjects which interested him he wrote more than one essay.

The letter form of the *Epistler* is a pleasant fiction. Holberg employed it because it was popular (e.g., in the moral weeklies) and because he wanted to write in an easy and familiar way, without paying too much attention to form, style, or academic demands. There is no standard to which a letter must adhere. Although Holberg's style in the *Epistler* is not always lucid, no doubt because of the speed with which some of the essays must have been written, his intent was to be perfectly clear and rational. A skilled writer of Danish, he makes no effort to be brilliant and, although he is humorous, he seldom turns a clever phrase. He speaks his mind and rarely insinuates. The simple, the clear, and the natural are for him representative of the divinely preordained condition of man, which man must seek to recapture. In contrast with Locke's famous concept of the *tabula rasa,* Holberg assumed the existence of absolute right and wrong and of duties which men are obliged to perform. He assumed a law in nature which is divinely established, a natural order which man is capable of comprehending and reproducing. This legacy of seventeenth century philosophy was noticeable in Holberg's *Introduction til Natur- og Folkeretten* ("Introduction to Natural and International Law") in 1716, and it was fundamental in the essays written thirty-five years later.

Although he was the apostle of the Enlightenment in Scandinavia, Holberg was no revolutionary spirit. He accepted the institutions of government as he knew them and was shocked by any attempt radically to change them. He was a loyal subject and citizen, inherently a conservative and a monarchist. As indicated in *Niels Klim,* his ideal of a state was in the last analysis the Danish state of the early eighteenth century, cleansed of any glaring blemishes or superficial and ephemeral faults. Holberg accepted the traditional Christian religion shorn of all fanaticism. His theological criticism left the basic dogma of Protestantism untouched—but then, so did Bayle's. Holberg was an apologist not so much for the *status quo* as for conditions which obtained about 1720 and for the philosophy of about 1700. He was skeptical of innovations and a critic of the new taste, particularly in the theater toward the middle of the century. His ideal of the drama was his own drama. While he preached tolerance in all things, he was convinced that his own works and his own opinions were fundamentally right. His objectivity was therefore somewhat of a delusion.

Holberg was very different from his renowned fellow countrymen of the next century, Kierkegaard and Grundtvig, both of whom loved the paradox and both of whom troubled clear waters. Unlike them, Holberg is not significant for his profoundness, but rather for having been a sensitive instrument that recorded the currents of the times. He transformed, reworked, and interpreted, as an historian, an essayist, or a writer of comedy. At the same time, he possessed the genius of giving effective form to his subject matter. He was the dynamic Northern outpost of the *république des lettres.*

Holberg believed that great men, clear thinking, and the spirit of tolerance could give an entire nation, or indeed all of Europe, a new and better temper. For him, individuals, rather than abstract social movements, moulded the world pattern, and reason was more important than introspection. The essays are evidence enough of Holberg's conviction that an individual, using his talents and his intellect to good advantage, need not be intimidated by the complexity of existence, that man's intellectual curiosity should be indulged, and that it is not without value for one man to express his opinion.

SELECTED ESSAYS OF LUDVIG HOLBERG

THE THREAT OF A UNIVERSAL MONARCHY
EPISTLE 5

To * *[1]

THE UNUSUAL progress which Thamas Kublai Khan has made in the Orient and the incredible speed with which he has overrun the Grand Mogul's domain and acquired almost indescribable wealth has caused you some agitation. In your last letter you enquire whether a new universal monarchy is not to be feared because of such events. To this I reply that never have I felt the threat of a universal monarchy to be less serious than in our time and that in this connection I do not begrudge the good Kublai Khan further progress. As far as I am concerned, he is at liberty to conquer all of India as well as China and Japan. This does not frighten me nor have I given up my tithings yet, although I hear that he has reduced all ecclesiastical property and incomes; it is far from here to Persia. If the great domains which were established closer to us by Genghis Khan and Tamerlane caused no agitation, the growth of Persia should arouse still less excitement. When Asiatic realms begin to grow, they generally grow southward; the chronicles and in particular the history of the ancient Persian monarchy show that there can be no expansion to the north. Consequently, since the time of Darius and Xerxes, no Oriental monarch has tried to conquer the part of the world which we inhabit. If therefore you fear a universal monarchy which can reach to the north, you should fix your glance on certain powerful European states

[1] The perfunctory salutation "To**," and the complimentary close, "I remain, etc.," are omitted in the translations of subsequent Epistles.

which seem to want to expand more and more; for Europe cannot be conquered except by itself. Under present conditions no conquest is to be feared. Although a large comet has been seen, I cannot be made to concur in the opinion of some and believe that it signifies impending change in government, although I am otherwise acquiescent and allow the common people unlimited freedom in prophesying about all other occurrences. I say that Europe has nothing to fear except a European potentate, for experience teaches that the great Asiatic monarchies which have overrun the other parts of the world have stumbled whenever they have turned toward Europe, so that this part of the globe has become a *non plus ultra* for them. On the other hand, Europe has been endangered by one or another European potentate who, since the fall of the Roman empire, has grown stronger. In his time Charlemagne was looked upon as a comet foreboding a universal domination. That emperor reigned over all of Italy, France, and Germany, and his power was so great that had they all been united, the other European states could not have counterbalanced it. Fears were dispelled at his death and the universal monarchy was stifled at birth. There were two contributing reasons: first, that his successor seemed by nature to be qualified rather as a priest than as a king and, second, that to Europe's good fortune it was an accepted custom of the times to divide an entire kingdom among the royal princes, a custom which Charlemagne's son and successor, Louis, observed. The great realm was divided into several kingdoms which soon made war upon one another—and Europe thus regained its balance.

The Ottoman empire has agitated Europe from time to time. Mohammed II was a frightening phenomenon for several years. Into what a fright he threw most European countries can be deduced from the general rejoicing that his death occasioned, and from the services of thanksgiving which were held in Christian churches on account of his demise. Some of his successors, in particular Solyman II, advanced still closer to us. That monarch appeared with a large and belligerent army in Germany; it is credible that he would have gone still farther if there had not at the same time arisen another European power which could hold Turkey in check. This power was Spain, which grew to such a degree under Charles V that all of Europe marveled. Charles was lord of Spain and the West Indies, the larger part of Italy, all of the Netherlands, and at the same time emperor in Germany. His troops were the most belligerent and best-disciplined of the times, and American riches enabled him to do everything. This threat, however, lasted only during two reigns. He himself had to yield when the leading states of Europe united against him. Even though Charles's realm was augmented with Portugal and her rich colonies in the East Indies, his son, Philip II, was unable to subjugate the United Provinces of the Netherlands, which were in revolt. In our own times, the French King Louis XIV agitated all of Europe. It seemed that France had not previously known her own strength, for hitherto she had always thought it necessary to seek the support of other rulers in order to hold the Austrian house in check. During the time of Louis XIV, France suddenly became the dismay of all Europe, so that there never had been a greater possibility of universal monarchy or at least never had been so much halloo about it. This was the more amazing since, at the beginning of Louis XIV's reign, the kingdom was no larger than it previously had been. This serves as proof of that king's great qualities, for neither before nor after has France presented such a spectacle. I am aware that many try to divest Louis XIV of his fame and ascribe the prestige which his kingdom enjoyed to the great generals and ministers of state who lived during his time, but it may be said that no kingdom can lack generals, ministers, and martial subjects under a ruler who appreciates skill and who by means of rewards encourages all to do their duty. For more than fifty years France not only carried on wars against the united forces of Europe but ended them honorably and to her own advantage. Every battle was for France a victory. It generally took but a few days to conquer the most powerful fortresses; and French seapower, which hitherto had enjoyed little prestige, grew so that it could hold both masters of the sea in check. In short the situation was so changed that confusion reigned in all nations. France's success was long ascribed to England's apathy, but even after England had entered into alliance with the enemies of France, it was evident that even this move had been of no avail. It was most remarkable that, although the reign of Louis XIV was an unbroken series of wars, the arts and sciences flourished under him as never before. No age known to history has produced so many learned men and great writers in one place, and no nation has brought forth greater works of art and more splendid buildings. France was thus at the same time the dismay and pride of all Europe. Persons of all nations flocked to Paris to see and hear what they had never seen nor heard before. Just as the kingdom surpassed all other countries in elegance, the court all others in *politesse,* and its academies all others in science and learning, the king surpassed all other men in appearance and physique. All travelers boasted of having seen Versailles, Fontainebleau, Marly, and other great works of architecture, but boasted still more of having seen the king's person, which, with regard to physique, majesty, and *politesse,* could be looked upon as nature's masterpiece. In short, everything combined at once to make France great and renowned, so that the name of France was hated, feared, and at the same time admired.

In this situation and under these difficult conditions Europe nevertheless retained its freedom, for with the King's increasing age everything in France seemed to age and decline. The hope of a fifth monarchy suddenly disappeared and the outcome of long and bloody wars was the emancipation of the country and the depletion of its inhabitants and wealth. The end result was nothing except distress and a gnawing conscience because several hundred thousand innocent human beings had been slaughtered in vain while the other subjects were left in utmost poverty.

From this you see, dear friend, that materials can be collected, timbers hewn, and scaffolding erected for a universal monarchy in our time, but that the building will hardly be completed and therefore that the fear which Kublai Khan's progress causes you is but a chimera. He may proceed before the wind southward, but if he turns his prow to the north he will be met by Russian and Turkish power, either of which is enough to keep him in check. I wonder that the growth of Russian power has not agitated you. Fear of Russia could at least have more semblance of a foundation, for here we see a domain which stretches from the Baltic almost to China, a great power at sea as well as on land, with well-disciplined, martial, and victorious soldiers who can endure more and be maintained at less cost than other European soldiers. This I say could cause you more serious reflections than the growth of the Persian empire, but I shall let the neighbors of Russia reflect on this matter, and in the interim I shall look upon the growth of Russia as a means eventually of overthrowing the Turkish rule which so long has disturbed Christendom. To be sure, Ottoman power is not impressive at present, but just as a single able ruler brought Russia, which previously was little respected, into its present estimable position, similarly a single reasonable ministry could make the Turkish state great and appalling, for a domain which comprises the most important countries of three continents, which has an abundance of money and aggressive soldiers, and which is ruled by emperors who have unlimited power, could create great excitement if it were put on another footing. Some years ago a grand vizier undertook to follow in the footsteps of Peter Alexiovich and to achieve for the Turkish state the same conditions which that great monarch had achieved for Russia. He endeavored to reform the militia and to introduce scholarship and science; he established presses in Constantinople, encouraged distinguished young Turkish gentlemen to travel abroad, and so forth, but this great undertaking collapsed with the death of that same vizier. His sad death aroused sympathy, but the neighbors of the Turks had no reason to grieve over it.

I remain, etc.

THE ENGLISH DEISTS AND THE STRUGGLE AGAINST THEM

EPISTLE 7

THE DEISTS in Great Britain continue to attack revelation and their boldness increases. It seems that the aversion which Englishmen have toward absolute power in civil government also extends to God's domain. It would seem that they wish to limit divine as well as royal power by Acts of Parliament, and that they will accept sovereignty neither in heaven nor on earth, for they have established societies to examine divine ordinances and rescripts in order to decide what should be accepted or rejected, and which articles are in conflict and which in accordance with the freedom of the English people. Since many theologians vigorously oppose the teachings and contentions of the freethinkers, there have now arisen in England two factions, called Whigs and Tories, which are far more significant than the old factions: The one party asserts the necessity of believing what God's revealed word demands; the other desires freedom to believe as it sees fit and to appeal to natural religion, as if revelation were a sort of lower court. Disputes are carried on vigorously by both parties, but it is not clear whether disputation is to the advantage or disadvantage of the church. Just as religion never before has been so severely attacked, it has at no time ever been so strongly defended. Since the Naturalists Collins, Tindal, Wholston, Morgan, and others employ new and hitherto almost unknown weapons in order to storm the fortresses of religion, its defenders have devised new fortifications. Current disputes are more troublesome than those with heretics because the Naturalists *excipere Forum* and place themselves under a different jurisdiction, so that their opponents must first convince them that there is no reason for *exceptio fori* and that both parties can meet on the same ground. In order to dispute to better advantage, the defenders of religion have found it wise to give up certain outworks in order better to protect the main redoubts. That is, they yield certain things that their forefathers held on to overzealously, in order to deprive the Naturalists of the opportunity to become involved in the sophistry and the complications to which an exaggerated orthodoxy leads. This has happened and is happening, with the desired results. The most significant of these concessions are: (1) To allow them freedom to examine the main tenets of religion and to dispute against them. This does away with the objection commonly advanced that by employing coercion and prohibition, orthodox believers make their religion suspect even as if they themselves doubted its truth; for it is averred that no one has a good case who will not let it be examined and that everyone who is certain of his right prefers arguments to force. (2) To depart from the literal interpretation of the Scriptures in certain matters. In the Scriptures many truths are represented by symbols, metaphors, and allegories which, if understood literally, can give rise to innumerable difficulties, but if looked upon as symbols, both strengthen the high opinion we have of the Scriptures' excellence and silence the critics of religion. For example, when God says to the prophet Hosea, "Go forth and marry a whore and beget two sons with her," we do not believe that this command is to be interpreted literally. It is to be understood symbolically in the sense that by a whore is meant the depraved Jewish church which the prophet is commanded to embrace and marry; for innumerable other passages testify that God abhors and forbids that which he seems here to command.

When we take into consideration that the style used in ancient times, and especially in the Orient, employed fables, metaphors, and allegories to represent important truths, we must then distinguish between that which is related in the

Scriptures and the way in which it is related or presented. Our theologians do not interpret literally when there is mention of God's hands, feet, entrails, etc., since it is obvious from other passages that He is a spirit. Then why not figuratively in other matters when necessary? I am aware that certain interpreters of the Scriptures have been severely criticized because they have explained some passage of a similar nature as an allegory. Critics who have interpreted the conversation between the serpent and Eve in Paradise as an allegory have been accused of unbelief and impiety. I do not dare here to take sides, but I would say that if these interpreters acted in good faith in order to silence the critics of religion, then the judgments which have been passed on them are far too harsh. I would be of the same opinion if similar explanations were forthcoming of the visits which the Devil is said to have paid to God and of their conversations regarding Job. If some one is of the opinion that the substance of the story is correct but the way in which it is told—true to the style of the times—is symbolic, I would not concur in passing harsh judgment on such an explanation, for I believe that even if these interpreters err, they err with a good design. He who, by writing commentaries, attempts to show the actual and fundamental meaning of a book cannot be accused of wanting to weaken or cast aspersions on it.

The third matter in which some modern theologians have found it necessary to give up contentions of their predecessors is that of the divine inspiration of Biblical authors. The inspiration they take to extend only to teachings but not to historical details or to style. They say that the law and the prophecies were dictated by God but that the history is based upon the reports of trustworthy men and that the style is the writers' themselves. By this limitation they have dulled the arrows of the unbeliever and have enabled themselves to refute his strongest objections. It is their opinion that no harm is done to the Scriptures if it be admitted that one book was written in better style and in a more orderly fashion than another and that history can be reliable even though all or a part of it may have been written by some one other than the author to whom it is ascribed. This they feel to be comparable to disrobing in order to preserve the body or sacrificing outworks in order to save a city. It is their intent to support the Scriptures to the same degree that others undermine them by defending untenable points uncompromisingly. If someone were to contend that the description of Moses's death and burial found in the book of Deuteronomy was written by Moses or the events which are recorded in the second book of Samuel but which took place long after Samuel's death were written by him, the entire history would be sacrificed and the enemy would be given cause for triumph.

The fourth concession is to admit occasional copyists' errors if necessity require it. Of what use is it to try to reconcile historical and chronological conflicts when they cannot be reconciled? This only arouses the contempt of one's enemies, who view such strained reasoning as sophistry. If, for example, a historian were to write that Alexander the Great ruled for twelve years but later in the same book were to write that he ruled fourteen years, we should have to admit that one figure is a copyist's error, otherwise it would seem that we were undertaking to conceal the truth and renounce the testimony of our own senses merely for the sake of defending a book; this would neither be proper for a Christian nor be in accord with Christ's teaching. I say, "when the necessity require it," since many are too ready to invoke copyists' errors in order to avoid racking their brains when confronted by some apparent paradox. What is more, it may be said that whoever would reconcile things that cannot be reconciled achieves nothing but the name of a partisan advocate, makes his whole case suspect, and is looked upon as a person who would renounce being a human in order to acquire the epithet of a zealous Christian. It is therefore that, in the present disputes with deists, some leading theologians are successfully employing moderation as an expedient.

On Freemasonry

Epistle 11

You write me that our common friend Theodoros has grown thin and emaciated since he entered the society of Freemasons. This does not surprise me, for what can be greater torment for a man whom nature has created full of chinks than to be bound to eternal silence, especially if the thing which he has sworn by oath to keep secret is, as quite plausibly may be the case, of little or no importance? I am convinced that this, rather than the papal excommunication, is the cause of his declining health. You request my opinion about the society of Freemasons and ask whether I am not able to guess its composition. That is just as difficult for me to guess as what will be the password that the city's military governor will issue tomorrow. Truthfully speaking, my curiosity has never been so great that I have tried to discover the secret. To be sure, the constant growth of the society might arouse considerable curiosity, especially since one notes that many eminent men let themselves be initiated into its mysteries and secrets. Since history shows that numerous similar secret societies have been established in the past and in the course of time have been found to be of no significance, I therefore look upon the society in question as upon the Rosicrucian Order of the previous century, which was nothing and became nothing. The most certain way to find out the society's secrets is to act as if one had no interest whatsoever in finding them out. It is plausible that the Freemasons are silent in order to arouse the curiosity of others. You know our Theodoros—act as if you do not care about knowing anything, then perhaps he will react like the girl in the comedy who said, "Now I will tell, just because you do not want to hear it." It is said that in order to insure perpetual silence, the Freemasons accept neither maid nor matron in their society. I thank the good men on behalf of the male sex and hope only that they will not be deceived in their high opinion of our sex. I can but congratulate the women of our times, for one observes that none of them are making the effort to pump their husbands on the subject. Nothing is easier for a clever woman than to loosen her husband's tongue and wheedle something out of him. Since the secret of the society has been kept to the present day, it has occurred to me that it must for that very reason be nonexistent. The resolutions and laws which the Freemasons accept must either be good or bad or be insignificant. If they are bad, it is incomprehensible that so many worthy and enlightened men should hesitate to break an obligation which is sinful and unlawful. If they are good, why are they held secret? No one can be without reproach who refuses to communicate to mankind whatever can be to its advantage and betterment. It is therefore reasonable to assume that this society was established solely for the sake of founding a society and arousing other people's curiosity; it serves no other function than to give people who have nothing to talk about a subject for conversation. There are various clubs and societies established in England for this purpose alone. Such undertakings can be compared to Alcibiades' cutting off his dog's tail. When his friends, who could not understand his act, asked the reason for it, he replied that it was only to give the Athenians a new subject for conversation. The Messrs. Freemasons should not consider this, my estimation, to be a satire since, rather, it is in defense of the society and shows that I ascribe to its members neither evil nor malignant design.

There now arises the important question whether such secret societies should be permitted. As is my wont, I here follow a middle path. On the one hand, I believe that the Pope has acted precipitously in putting the Freemasons under the ban of the Church, for to sentence to Hell men about whose deeds and achievements one has no idea is strange indeed, and such excommunication can therefore be looked upon as *fulmen brutum* which can have no effect. If the society of Freemasons consists only of a name and its members have nothing to do, one might well advise them, in order not to be entirely idle, to retaliate, and excommunicate the Pope and the cardinals; then the question would be which excommunication had the greater effect. On the other hand, I believe a government cannot be blamed which tries to discourage such societies, for secret meetings arouse suspicion and are therefore difficult to tolerate in any country. Although they can be beneficial and innocent, they nevertheless do give occasion to plots and conspiracies, of which we have numerous examples both in ancient and modern history.

MANDEVILLE'S *Fable of the Bees*
EPISTLE 21

AT MILORD'S request I have read Mandeville's work entitled *Fable of the Bees.* I readily admit that it is ingenious, but it is at the same time as ungodly as it is ill-founded. Although the author has been able to support his thesis with arguments difficult to refute, it would be discreditable and odious to preach the necessity of vice and to disseminate a doctrine through which men can be made worse than they are. On the other hand, one can say that the doctrine is so scandalous in itself and so poorly expounded that it can be refuted very easily. He bases his entire work on a fable about the bees in order to demonstrate the necessity of vice and immorality. There is represented a beehive in which bees lived in great abundance of everything. At the same time the bees were given to all sorts of vices, such as avarice, extravagance, pride, envy, vanity, etc. The bees at last grew tired of the difficulties which arose from this state of affairs and sought a remedy. Jupiter heard their plea and caused Mercury to expel all their vices and, instead, to introduce an equal number of virtues. Through this act the republic of the bees immediately took on a different appearance. Prices fell, judges and lawyers had nothing more to do, the courts stood vacant,—in short, commerce, trade, and the arts and sciences stagnated.

This caused the beehive to fall into a state of extreme poverty so that the bees finally fled from it and into a hollow tree where nothing of their previous prosperity remained but where they lived in constant virtue and penury. The author gives lengthy explanations for the change in circumstances, and endeavors to show the necessity of vice for the well-being and preservation of a society. I shall omit citing the arguments with which he attempts to support this dangerous paradox and mention only one thing whereby one can judge the rest. He says that thievery is also beneficial and that when one steals a thousand pounds from a rich man it is of just as great advantage to society as if an archbishop were to bequeath or give an equal sum to the poor, since the money in both cases comes into the hands of common people and brings activity to society.

It will readily be admitted that a city like London or Amsterdam which, with regard to commerce, wealth, and the number of inhabitants, is considered to be flourishing, would, like the above-mentioned beehive, lose its reputation (although not be brought to a state of poverty) if avarice, luxury, rancor, etc., ceased all at once. The question remains whether society would be the worse for the change; the question remains whether that society can be called flourishing where certain citizens assemble great riches and treasures which become only a burden to them while others live in the utmost poverty. Yet this is the condition generally prevailing in all the so-called flourishing cities now looked upon as the ornaments of the earth. One observes all the inhabitants of these cities living in continuous thraldom and constant anxiety: the rich are plagued by fear and the poor by envy, so that one does not know whom to pity most—those who have too much or those who have too little. If in wealthy and powerful cities you find many works of art and magnificent buildings, then you also find many whipping posts, gallows, and wheels of torture. Let us imagine two societies, the one like that of the ancient Essenes, Gymnosophists, etc., the other made up of the so-called respectable citizens now found in the most esteemed European cities: In the one you will find sensible people in everyday clothes and small dwellings, in the other wild and pernicious animals, below a surface of ostentation. The first are pleasing to the eyes of a philosopher, the second to the eyes of vain persons. The first are healthy kernels under a coarse exterior, the second rotten kernels in a pretty shell. One must not judge man's nature by exterior appearance; wealth, buildings, works of art, commerce, and several sciences serve rather as a proof of deplorable conditions and unhappiness. The fortifications of a city signify fear of an enemy. Many sciences which are pursued with zeal lay bare the vanity of man, and every splendid city hall is a disfiguration like a boil upon the human body. If on the outside you find gilding, marble, carving, and other ornamentation, then inside you find instruments of torture, prisons, and other evidence that the city in general is of little worth.

It can be objected that everything which I value so little is useful and necessary in mankind's present state and that a society which renounced these inanities would be oppressed with little or no difficulty by their mighty neighbors. Ships and fleets are built for the sake of commerce; commerce is carried on in order to acquire wealth; wealth is acquired in order to support troops in times of war; and cities are fortified in order not to be taken by storm. There is an element of necessity in all of this, and one can therefore maintain that the welfare and security of a society is promoted *in statu quo* by vice and vanity. To the objection a double answer can be given, first, that I am not thinking of a specific society but of society in general. The question is not whether it is advisable to renounce riches and the means through which riches are acquired and so to weaken a society by voluntary poverty that it might be exploited by men of evil intent. The question is not whether it is advisable to be unarmed among thieves. It is rather whether vice and imperfections further the welfare and happiness of mankind—and this we can by no means say to be the case. When all societies exile imperfection and vice, then that which in mankind's present depraved condition is held to be prosperity will be transformed into misery, and that which is held to be ornamental, transformed to disfiguration. It is therefore bad to decree the necessity of vice in general, as Mr. Mandeville seems to do. Even if he states that this is not his intent, and that he bases his thesis alone upon the depraved condition of mankind, and that it is necessary to howl with wolves, to steal with thieves, and to plunder with brigands, one can, holding strictly to his thesis, reply that a society without imperfections and vice could not only defend itself against others but also live forever in a state of well-being, security, and freedom.

The work of the Spartan legislator Lycurgus shows that a country without such evils, the necessity of which Mandeville preaches, not only can defend itself against others but also acquire prestige. In Sparta no one was concerned with saving money, for it was of no use. The contempt for money served to do away with disputes and lawsuits, envy, hate, and other vices. In short, the city did not at all correspond to the model in Mr. Mandeville's catechism and should therefore have been considered to be of no consequence. Yet, for all its poverty and its ignorance of many sciences, Sparta not only defended itself against its neighbors, but was looked upon as the queen of Greek cities. Since the Spartans showed no desire to extend the boundaries of their community, they not only remained unattacked by their neighbors but were chosen as judges in disputes between other Greek cities, and Sparta came to be looked upon as a common tribunal for all of Greece. Nothing induced the other Greeks to carry on offensive wars against men who renounced political superiority and riches, the very tinder of war and hostility. If anyone had wanted to attack the city, he would upon approaching it have found brave citizens jealous of their honor who, young and old, would have died with sword in hand. Yes, in conquering the city one would have gained nothing except some small houses and huts and some few copper coins which were used instead of gold and silver. Despite its poverty, its ignorance of most Greek sciences, and its lack of external ornamentation, Sparta was nevertheless respected, flourishing, strong—yes, almost unconquerable. It was safe from external enemies, since no one could or would attack it. It was free from internal strife, since there was no reason for dispute. The city was respected and honored because it exercised impartiality and justice over the Greeks. Indeed, it had acquired superiority precisely because it had not sought superiority. A society like that of Sparta can be said truly to thrive. The conditions described here lasted several centuries or until the Spartans began to abandon the virtues of their forefathers and to open the gates of the city to the vices which Mr. Mandeville feels to be necessary for the sake of a nation's might and prosperity. The city did not begin to diminish before it tried to expand. One concludes that Mr. Mandeville's doctrine of the necessity of vice for the welfare of a state is an unfounded paradox. The virtues which produced security, prosperity, and prestige for the Spartans have the same effect in other societies, and could perhaps be still more successful if the social institutions were better than those of Lycurgus.

I readily admit that several arts and sciences would die out along with the faults and vices. Quarrelsomeness and disputes *de meo* & *tuo* are essential to the law and have furnished niceties for judicial study. Man's disorderly living, which causes sickness, has advanced medicine. Violence and malice have taught us to raise fortresses and to fortify cities and to make mathematical sciences more intricate daily. Pride has built palaces, even churches and hospitals, and has given birth to architecture. Avarice has instructed in navigation, taught us to build ships, and brought us knowledge of distant and unknown countries, etc. But all these advantages exist only in the imagination and are based alone on a sort of necessity brought forth by the evil inclinations of man; for when vices cease, these so-called necessary sciences and studies become nothing but words, and things of no significance. As soon as disputes cease, juridical study is no longer of consequence—and is it a disaster if some hundred barristers are transformed into an equal number of husbandmen? The same can be said about other sciences. If sicknesses which arise from disorderly living ceased, it would be useless to study certain phases of medicine. It is the same with fortifications and architecture, which no longer can be reckoned among the arts when hostility, pride, and vanity depart. As far as seamanship is concerned, I gladly admit that it is agreeable to acquire knowledge by sailing to strange and distant countries and that therefore this skill never can be said to be useless, but the skill need not cease because of virtue. One could continue to sail to foreign places in order to acquire knowledge about them. This could become the single purpose of such journeys, whereas the purpose now is almost entirely to seek riches and to return home with unnecessary, indeed often unwholesome wares. Nature has sufficiently provided each country with the products which it needs and the goods which are the most valuable for its inhabitants. Finally it should be remarked that, if men were free from unnecessary occupations and if skills were fewer, men would make greater and more perfect progress in the skills which remained. The branches of knowledge which would be cultivated in that state of innocence would be theology, physics, astronomy, agriculture, and others which edify the mind, benefit mankind, and preserve life and health. Under such conditions there would be better theologians and better naturalists than there are at present or there now can become. The entire earth, of which a large part lies fallow because of men's other occupations and a lack of husbandmen, would be transformed into a garden and bear more and better fruits. In short, one would find highly skilled instead of half-skilled persons in various branches of knowledge. They who now touch the bark of the matter would penetrate to its pith. When one considers all this, he concludes that Monsieur Mandeville's thesis is bad and ill-founded. One may remark that if he is not a better doctor of medicine than of morals it would be precarious to take his cure.

of Ludvig Holberg

Jean Le Clerc as a Theologian

Epistle 32

In his last communication Milord mentions that he has read with pleasure Jean Le Clerc's commentaries on the Holy Scriptures but remarks that he is in disagreement with much the author says, since Le Clerc often is presumptuous in his expositions and casts doubt on certain miracles. Since I follow Philipp Melanchthon's principle that men of good intent can err, I pass less severe judgment on Le Clerc than many others do. I have read all his works and can from them conclude nothing but that he was a good Christian despite all the errors which are ascribed to him and which he possibly can have made. I have the same opinion about the great Grotius in whose footsteps he followed. Both these worthy men have with the best of intentions undertaken reasoned expositions of the Holy Scriptures; to this end they first acquainted themselves with Greek and Hebrew and then, after having put their prejudices and the expositions of others aside, sought to deduce the true meaning of the Scriptures on the basis of grammatical and generally accepted critical rules. One must admit that such intent is commendable. Nevertheless, everyone who proceeds in this manner will be forced to relinquish some generally accepted explanation, especially since older expositors had little or no knowledge of Hebrew and were therefore not so skilled in interpreting the Bible as the scholars of our own times who are well-grounded in Greek and Hebrew and are expert in the art of criticism. Two Jewish rabbis, Avenares and Maimonides, came to conclusions which did not correspond to those of other rabbis, since both of them undertook to expound the Scriptures according to grammatical rules.

Milord censures Le Clerc because he, like Grotius, casts doubt on certain prophecies which are considered to refer to the Messiah. I do not approve of these his expositions, although I am convinced that neither he nor Grotius explained away certain prophecies save with the intent of strengthening others. They believed that nothing weakens religion more than the attempt to force words to mean something which is impossible according to all rules of grammar and exposition, and that the employment of arguments which are untenable only gives the enemies of religion the opportunity to consider all other explanations partisan and untrustworthy. When a man admits that certain interpretations are not well-founded, his testimony in other matters carries still more weight. The same can be said of miracles. To what advantage is it to act as if certain natural phenomena were miracles? This serves only to arouse doubt about the true miracles. That both Le Clerc and Grotius worked for the best of the Christian religion can be deduced from their profound works on the truth of the Christian faith. There is adequate evidence in his other writings that Le Clerc was a champion of the Christian religion in general. His writings attest a remarkable power of discernment and his life is ample evidence that he renounced all wealth and worldly dignity so that he might write freely and bring to light what he felt to be the truth. He lived almost in poverty and worked for Dutch publishers in order to earn his daily bread. It would therefore be unjust to pass harsh judgment on such a man. Since the beginning of Christianity, no time has been more full of heresies than ours, for we see insidious men each year bring forth works against religion in general, not in order to dispute some articles of faith as formerly was the case, but to attack the very fundamentals of faith and to assault its bulwarks. In such times Christian sects should put aside internal differences and mutual distrust, in order to unite their forces against a common enemy, after the fashion of political parties which form a coalition when necessary for a common defense. Under these critical circumstances it is requisite not stubbornly to defend some chance opinion but to employ only arguments which are significant and irrefutable. This has been the design of Grotius, Le Clerc, and other moderate theologians. By means of reasonable arguments, they have sought to put the Scriptures above all criticism. They have not stressed interpretations which lack substance, and they have abandoned interpretations which are unreliable in order not to give the enemies of revelation occasion for satire. Finally, they have regularly urged concord and mutual tolerance upon those, who, although in agreement about the fundamental articles of faith, are separated by petty differences. It is by such means that the bulwarks of religion best can be defended. The theologians of all sects must necessarily employ these means if the Naturalists continue as they have begun. Time will perhaps show that this my prophecy is not ill-founded and that the unity which hitherto has been sought in vain will be brought about by present exigencies, so that syncretists like Grotius, Le Clerc, and others will be looked upon as the pillars of religion, while the choleric theologians will be dismissed as the incompetent militia of the church militant.

Bayle's Dictionary

Epistle 34

You criticize our common friend C. A. for reading so much in Bayle's works. I for my part do not blame him for this, since, although there are found various objectionable things in Bayle's writings, it must nevertheless be admitted that one can profit much from that author's works and in particular escape a taste for the trivial with which most academic people are infected. In Bayle's writings one always finds something that is new and unusual. Although some of his opinions are not acceptable, they nevertheless give occasion to enquire into various things which otherwise would not occur to everyone. No author either old or new who is known to me has written with greater pithiness and penetration, and no publication has appeared which, with regard to zeal, accuracy, variety of material, thorough criticism, and gallant style, can be compared with his critical Dictionary. In it one finds a profound philosophy, a searching analysis of all sorts of matters, and an unusual accuracy—even in the most minute details—which would not be expected in such an extensive work, and especially in an author who writes like a gentleman and therefore cannot be expected to observe such accuracy and to have his thoughts devoted to names, dates, etc. Every page in the Dictionary gives evidence of endless and almost slavish reading. If it is history that is in question, one notes that nothing has escaped him; he has read everything, important and unimportant, that might serve to enlighten and in addition correct the mistakes of others. In the case of philosophy, one observes that he not only has studied thoroughly all the old as well as new philosophical systems but is able to make thorough, unusual, and original comments about them. With what pithiness he writes can be seen from the fact that, although no teachings have been considered easier to refute than the Manichæic and Skeptic, Bayle has nevertheless so glossed them over that the great theologians and philosophers have had to unite their forces in order to combat his thesis. In short, his Dictionary gives evidence of hard work, of painstaking, and of an unusual penetration and discernment. When one considers the work's extensiveness —to wit, that it consists of four large folios which, printed in ordinary type, could fill eight volumes—one must say that this is a work which exceeds one man's powers. The peculiar paradoxical opinions which he scatters about have brought him many powerful enemies. That they blame him for such opinions is excusable, but when his enemies pretend that his writings are full of gossip and confusion, they manifest only their own animosity. I for my part read no writings with greater admiration. It does not strike me as strange, therefore, that our friend, since he has good taste, reads so much in them.

of Ludvig Holberg

A Projected Limitation of Armaments

Epistle 39

I THANK YOU for your letter in which you report that you recently attended a meeting of a society in the country which you call the *Collegium Politicum*—and there are more societies of this nature in the provinces than in large cities. You mention that among other political matters the following question was debated: What can be the cause of the great lack of public funds in all countries, although all rulers' incomes are incomparably greater than they were a century ago? This is an important and interesting question but, as you say, the answers or guesses which have been made do not solve the problem. The principal reason appears to me to be that rulers employ more soldiers and entertain greater military establishments than the countries can tolerate. Formerly, countries carried on prolonged wars, although the amount raised by taxation was less, whereas now after two or three years of war there is talk of lack of funds—even in France where the royal revenues are greater by many millions than they were a century ago. There might be named several subordinate reasons, but the actual reason for such debility is the size of the armies, which are out of proportion to the various nations' resources. Petty princes now put in the field as many troops as the most powerful kings in former days. It is therefore no wonder that treasuries are emptied quickly, for no augmentation of income can make up for the increase in expenditures. Consequently, all rulers will continue to suffer from a shortage of funds in times of war if former conditions are not restored and each nation's troops reduced to their former number. I take the liberty of communicating to you a plan which I have developed that might bring this about. I submit it with the request that it be carefully examined in the political college; here in Copenhagen I shall mention it to no one, in part because the city is full of satirical persons who perhaps would say the Abbé de St. Pierre's dreams were beginning to be revived, and in part because city dwellers do not have the same insight into affairs of state as villagers who would rather neglect their morning and evening prayers than their newspaper reading and are therefore the better judges in political matters.

My suggestion is this: A general law or *conclusum* could be made with the assent of all Christian rulers—and if the Turkish emperor would subscribe to it so much the better—to the effect that every ruler in times of war should not put more than a certain number of troops in the field, a number determined by a general European commission according to the resources and size of the nation. The consequence would be that wars would not be half as costly as they are now and every ruler could have more select and better-disciplined troops and would not be forced to hire as many mercenaries as now is the case in order to save his country from becoming bereft of inhabitants. I have no doubt but that your political society will immediately make several objections and will say among other things: What will become of the Swiss and other peoples that depend on hiring out mercenaries? Is it right to deprive whole nations of their honest living? But, my friend, if the members of our political college raise such an objection, please be good enough to make clear to them how unjust it is to reject such a useful suggestion solely for the sake of encouraging some mountain dwellers' commerce. Furthermore, the livelihood of the Swiss will not be impaired, for Savoy, the Italian states, and others will continue to employ their soldiers as before. This my suggestion does not forbid employing such troops in so far as the numbers involved are in proportion to each country's resources and wealth. To a certain extent the Swiss can also profit from it, for if there are fewer troops to remunerate, payments will be more regular, so that it will no longer be *point d'argent, point des Suisses.*

The other objections which I imagine will be made are these: It will be said, first, that rulers will not let themselves be bound but on the contrary will use all the force which is at their disposal. To this may be replied that no one is bound if the agreement is voluntary and no one can find an arrangement disagreeable which saves both so much money and so many subjects while each state remains quite as powerful and important as it was before. For example, France presumably supports 300,000 men-in-arms in times of war. This number is held to be necessary because the enemies of France can put an equal force into the field. Both sides are discomfited by having to support such great armies. If a general reduction were made according to my plan so that the size of an army were in proportion to the size of the country, 100,000 men would be just as significant for France as 300,000 men are now. The annual costs of supporting 200,000 men would be saved and the country would, so to speak, still have the same military power as before. If two persons grapple with one another, each will use all five fingers, but if the agreement is made that only one finger is to be used, this finger becomes quite as important in the contest as the five might be. In olden days entire nations settled disputes by letting ten or twelve champions from each camp meet in combat. Under such an arrangement twelve men were as important as 100,000. No one's power is limited by such an arrangement, for every nation would accomplish with one-third of its military forces what it now accomplishes with all three-thirds. The second objection will doubtless be that, as attractive as this plan might seem and as useful as it might be, we can conclude from experience that unanimous consent to the plan would be almost impossible to obtain, for although it does not actually limit, it nevertheless seems to limit a ruler's power. And should one ruler refuse to subscribe to such a pact, the entire arrangement would be useless. To this I reply, first, that it is not credible that anyone would refuse to agree to a suggestion the common value of which is so obvious and, second, that in case some ruler should not subscribe, the pact could be made among those rulers who perceive its usefulness. They would mutually observe a proportion of military strength but might employ all the strength at their command against the dissenters. When the latter saw the advantages of the agreement and noted that the treasuries of the former were well supplied when their own were empty, one dissenter after the other would join the league and readily agree to that which he previously had rejected. The third objection would presumably be that, although all rulers agreed to subscribe to such a pact, one of them would try secretly to break it if he saw that a coup might be made quickly. To this I reply that it is impossible greatly to increase a military establishment and have it remain unnoticed by all and that when the action of the recalcitrant ruler was discovered, he would immediately be excluded from the league, and the other rulers could increase their forces as they saw fit against him as a violator both of a treaty and of international law.

In short, when three or four rulers unite to this end the rest will follow. I shall elucidate with an example. Assume that France and Spain are at war. France can support 100,000 men as easily as Spain 40,000. The number of troops from both countries is regulated according to the respective country's resources. If it is objected that 40,000 Spaniards cannot defend themselves against 100,000 Frenchmen, I would point out that the Spanish monarch, like all lesser potentates, must seek his strength in alliances with other nations if he is not to become the booty of a mightier enemy. That the number of troops is limited is inconsequential, since each nation would be proportionately as strong as it is now. If Spain exerted herself to the utmost and increased the number of her troops to 80,000, France would put 160,000 men into the field. The only difference would be that, according to my plan, both countries could carry on a war at lesser cost, as in the days before nations began to increase their military establishments out of proportion to their resources and wealth. When other rulers who do not belong to the league observe that the two nations in question still have full treasuries after a prolonged war, indeed that they are strengthened rather than weakened by such a war, since their soldiery has become hardened to warfare, whereas on the other hand countries who carry on wars in the now customary fashion are stripped both of inhabitants and funds, they will themselves request admission to the league in order to obtain the advantages it offers. A fourth objection might be that a nation does not suffer as much as imagined by supporting a large army; the treasury is emptied, to be sure, but money circulates and passes from the hands of patricians and landed gentry into the hands of soldiers and merchants. In order to be convinced of the opposite, one has but to observe the miserable conditions into which nations have been plunged by prolonged wars. Think only of the deplorable state of France during the prolonged War of the Spanish Succession, when for lack of funds the government was ready to give *carte blanche* in order to save the country from total destruction. It should here be noted that during such wars large amounts of money leave the country.[a]

Dear friend, do not forget to explain all this to your political brethren, should they raise such objections against my plan. It would please me greatly if the plan found favor with such sensible statesmen, for their approbation could only give me hope of success. They may take the credit for the plan. I shall be satisfied if I have been able to better the common weal by good counsel. I await your opinion in the matter.

Life in a Town and Life in the Country

Epistle 41

You write me that you have sold your country estate and intend to establish yourself in the nearest town. If you are doing this for the sake of peace and quiet, I fear that you have made a mistake; he who would live a quiet life should take

[a] Some time after this was written I heard that some person unknown to me really made such a suggestion, but under what circumstances I do not know.

up his residence either in the country or in a capital city, for in both these places one is free to philosophize as much as one will, in the country because one is alone and in the capital because one can be alone. The larger the city, the greater the freedom. In London, Paris, and Rome it is possible to live, so to speak, in retreat, as I can demonstrate by my own example. For this reason Descartes sought out large cities, that he could meditate unhindered. Everyone looks out for himself in populous places, so that one man does not know what the next man is doing. In small towns, on the other hand, it is quite different. There a person becomes known right away, and is enquired about and criticized. Everyone is at once acquainted with your state of mind, present condition, and habits, and it becomes common knowledge what you do at home, when you rise and retire, when you dine, what you eat and drink, etc. What is more, the smaller towns are generally divided into factions, so that even without willing it a person becomes a Tory or a Whig, a Guelf or a Ghibelline. To try to be neutral is to be between two fires or to be considered a misanthrope or a night owl. I imagine therefore that your intent in taking up residence in a small town is rather to have an opportunity to participate in affairs of state and justice, for such places are the true schools of politics and law here in this country. This I know by experience, for in whatever house I have come, I have been regaled with such subjects, and every library I have seen consists of law books, ordinances, and volumes of old newspapers that go back to the times of Henrik Gøde and Christian Cassube. It is easy to conclude that people who have the contents of all these volumes in their heads must be able politicians. From experience we also know that most legislative projects have their origins in such places and many persons who come from the provinces feel themselves capable of reforming the capital. What cannot constant reading and practice lead to? When the day's mail has arrived you will hear of nothing but marches, countermarches, battles, besieged cities, and other foreign affairs real and imaginary. On these days there is no innkeeper who can give me a tankard without saying, "It looks bad for the emperor" or "It looks bad for France"—or something similar. As far as legal procedure is concerned, they are so skilled in formalities that every citizen can go to court and defend his own case without the help of an attorney. I dare say that the inhabitants of small towns are better jurists than politicians. Law is their principal study and greatest pleasure. I have been told that a certain man who lived in such a place was cured of a quartan fever when, after not having carried on a lawsuit for a long time, he saw two summoners on his property. When I am in the capital I live quite nonchalantly and pay no particular attention in speaking or in writing letters, but when I have to do with villagers I weigh every word before I speak and consider every letter before I put it on paper so that no one can find cause for criticism, for with them the omission of a comma or a period can occasion a lawsuit. I say this in order to point out the accuracy and learning of villagers; I know that the inhabitants of larger towns are no match for them.

If therefore you have chosen your new residence in order to pursue the branches of learning mentioned above, you have done well to seek a place where they flourish. If, on the other hand, you seek only tranquillity, you will perhaps repent your decision. I have not been able to keep myself from communicating to you these my reflections.

Who Should Teach Theology?

Epistle 45

Some time ago a certain man known to Milord whispered in my ear these words: *ne sutor ultra crepidas;* and therewith went away without further explanation. I later had an opportunity to ask him what he meant by the admonition, and he said that I was a dabbler in writing about theological matters from which I should hold myself aloof and which I should rather leave to ecclesiastics, who were concerned with them by profession. To this I answered that I had written nothing theological unless it were in connection with certain moral subjects which I have discussed and which are so closely related to theology that they cannot be separated from it. This gave me the opportunity to point out to him the common misconception which people have when they assume that no one can be capable of instructing, or should be authorized to instruct, in theology except those who wear the livery of the Christian church and who are salaried for instructing in it. It was my opinion that men who had not by oath bound themselves to defend certain accepted and prevailing opinions were the best fitted to act as teachers, and I cited Erasmus, Grotius, Clericus, and others, who, although not clergymen, nevertheless with their expositions of the Scripture have thrown light upon many things and revealed many truths which ecclesiastics accept and follow. When one gives a clergyman a problem to solve, he is obliged to answer, "As far as my office permits." If, on the other hand, one consults with another learned man, he answers, "As far as I have investigated and am able to comprehend." Skillful as Æneas Sylvius was to teach and instruct before he became pope, the more awkward he became after his advancement to that high office. It's dignity lay like a heavy fog before his eyes, so that which Æneas had observed to be crooked and awry, Pius II found to be straight and orderly. He and many others have fared like the man who observed many mistakes of the city council before he himself became a member of it, whereupon he changed his tune, saying, "I would not have believed that all went so well in the council before I myself became a burgomaster." If one wants to have the most reliable information about a matter, one should preferably listen to the remarks of a man who has investigated but is not involved in it, rather than to those of an advocate who already has taken sides in the matter. My criticism is not at all intended to demonstrate clergymen's inability to teach, but only to reply to those who believe that learned persons who do not hold ecclesiastical office are unfitted and not entitled to teach. Common sense tells us that he whose only occupation is to meditate and who renounces all other business, must necessarily be more adept at solving problems ecclesiastical as well as secular than men who, having been sworn into office, are bound to the particular system of religion accepted in their countries. It is obvious that many systems of religion are based upon special interest and worldly authority and not at all upon Christ's teachings and common sense. It is credible therefore that, as a certain theologian says, if the Apostles came to earth, they would not understand a particle of the theology which is taught in certain places, as for example at Conimbra and Salamanca.

The Best Place to Live

Epistle 48

I see from your last communication that you intend to leave your fatherland and establish yourself in some foreign place where you think that you might spend the rest of your life with greater satisfaction. You complain of various evils which reign among your countrymen, such as hate, envy, pride, quarrelsomeness, etc. I am willing to admit that your complaints may be well founded, but, if you imagine you can find some other place which is free from the same evils, you are deceiving yourself. I have heard of a man who left his fatherland with an intent the same as yours and established himself in a strange place. Shortly after his arrival he observed the Devil standing on the roof of the house which he had rented, whereupon he said, "Are you here too? If I had known that, I could just as well have remained in the land of my birth." He noticed before long that the evils which had vexed him in his own country reigned elsewhere too and therefore he journeyed home again. In addition you asked me, as a widely traveled man, which foreign country pleased me the most and where I would advise you to take up residence. I have heard Switzerland and particularly Geneva highly praised, especially since one can there be in the center of Europe and near France, Italy, and Germany. The inhabitants are considered to be good and honest people and it is said that everything is reasonably priced, but I can give no detailed account thereof, since I never have been there. I observe that you seek a place where the air is healthful. This is not unwise, although I believe that the air one is used to from childhood is the most healthful. Icelanders, Greenlanders, and the inhabitants of the coldest and dampest places in Norway are happier and healthier at home than abroad. People who wander from one place to another do so to no advantage to their health, in my opinion. He who in youth and manhood always has lived on a dunghill makes no mistake if he remains there in his old age. Constant travel and change of air do not agree with everyone as well as with the shoemaker of Jerusalem who, after 1,700 years' wandering, is said still to be in good health. But you would doubtless intend to remain at some agreeable, pleasant, and healthful place after once establishing yourself there. If you persist in executing your plan then it is best that you seek advice from those who are familiar with Geneva.

Of all the countries I have been in, none please me more than Flanders and Brabant, but since most European wars seem to germinate there, these countries also have their disadvantages. Aside from that, however, I have found much that is agreeable there and, if I were required to dwell abroad, I would choose Brussels as my place of residence. The inhabitants there are just as courteous as the Parisians but are more reliable, do not have so many affectations, and make less noise. For less money I can make almost as much of my time there as in Paris and, if I want to travel, I can in eight days view over fifty large and splendid towns. Everywhere in the Netherlands there are good cobblestone roads. Barges transport me from one place to another so that whether I travel by land or by water, the journeys are agreeable. What has pleased me the most in traveling through these countries is that I have been able to spend every night in a town of considerable size, and that of an evening I have been able to go to the opera or the theater directly upon arrival by carriage. One appreciates the nobility of these provinces best if one comes directly from France and has made one's way over bad roads and through noxious towns with a low and disagreeable coach and, in addition, has had to bargain with innkeepers for every mouthful of food one wants. In England there is great freedom, and good food and drink, but the common people are haughty and look upon strangers as werewolves or semi-human beings. With regard to the neatness of towns and buildings, Holland has much that can please the eye, but the country is not healthful. To take up residence there is like living on a comet, for everything is filled with fog and tobacco smoke. Germany is very similar to the Scandinavian countries, so that you will not find any remarkable differences there. In Italy there are many annoying people, and in Spain you must be prepared to live on air alone. In short, every country has its disadvantages, a fact which, if you consider it carefully, may cause your "travel fever" to disappear. That our youth does not want to stay at home I can understand fairly well, for that age is flighty and full of quicksilver. It seems furthermore that our young Scandinavian gentlemen cannot long endure to keep their patrimony which they feel to be all too heavy a burden and which they can rid themselves of quickly by traveling abroad. But at your age such an undertaking will be more severely criticized; it will be said: *stulti locum mutant.* Think how difficult it is to move one's possessions to distant countries, specifically how many contingencies one may suffer on the way. Peder Paars undertook a journey of but twelve miles and over such a short distance he had so many adventures that he had material enough for a book in four parts. A wise man of your age left the country some years ago in order to settle in the East Indies. By so doing he thought he could lengthen his life—but he died immediately after his arrival in Tranquebar, so that he made the long and difficult journey only to die somewhere else. That many Jews travel to the Holy Land in their old age in order to be buried there is to be ascribed to a religious principle, since they believe that the resurrection will occur only in that country and that they who die elsewhere must come in a subterranean fashion thither. Others believe that it makes no difference in what land one dies, if one but die saved. I hope that you will take my admonition into consideration, although it is a mixture of pleasantry and earnest.

An Apology for the Devil

Epistle 60

Our last conversation concerned apologies, or vindications, for which I admitted a dislike, in part because an honest man and a good book require no apology—the man's life and the book's contents vindicate themselves—in part because it is possible to write a defense of anything including the Devil himself. You laughed at my remark and said that this would probably be rather difficult. To this I replied that it would be no more difficult to compose than the vindication of the donkey in which various heroic qualities are ascribed to that animal.

In order to show that it is possible I shall briefly sketch what an apologist, would he make the effort, could say in defense of the Devil. I shall not speak of his mental capacity and intellect, for even his worst enemies are in agreement that a person who has almost 6,000 years behind him and has lived twice as long as the shoemaker of Jerusalem must possess more learning and wisdom than all Seven Wise Men of Greece, indeed perhaps more than all the professors in the world put together, unless it be assumed that the Devil is in his second childhood; but that is a matter which no one save a physician can determine, since the most learned theologians who have studied the Devil's character and who know him like a book are aware that he still is enjoying his full vigor and that old age has had little or no effect on him. The learned men, who in the foregoing century had the honor of speaking with the shoemaker of Jerusalem, have witnessed that that same shoemaker was still enjoying his five senses and lacked neither comprehension nor memory, although he had wandered about in the world for 1,600 years. There can therefore be no debate regarding the Devil's intellect and learning which, because of his great age, can be nothing but vast. It is for this reason that the Norwegian peasants honor him with the venerable title of Old Erik.

Now let us examine the vices with which he is charged. The Devil is said constantly to be trying to bring misfortune to human beings and to beguile souls. But since he openly and as it were by manifesto has declared war on the human race, he is more to be excused than many people who under the guise of friendship deceive their neighbor, make pacts and agreements which they at once break, and call upon God to witness their righteous hearts, which nevertheless are full of hatred, animosity, and avarice. There is good reason for the saying: one can beware of the Devil but not of man. That he tries to beguile souls is no more than an attempt to increase his power and to prove that he is a clever politician, statesman, and economist. He is more dependable in pacts and contracts than most people, for they make pacts only to break them, and have so discredited themselves that a contract no longer is acceptable unless it is strengthened by another's guarantee. Experience teaches that the Devil keeps his agreements to the letter, does precisely what he has promised the contracting party, and seizes no one before the stipulated time is up. This is demonstrated by Dr. Faust and other honorable men, whom he agreed to teach arts, learning, and statesmanship or to aid with large subsidies, and from whom he asked no payment for his labors until the last minute of the last hour of the stipulated time had passed. For all the evil said about the Devil, one never hears of his having been accused of breach of contract nor of his having deceived anyone with counterfeit money or counterfeit wares as many of our merchants and authors now do, the former by giving their wares misleading names, the latter by giving their works misleading titles for the sake of subscription. The Devil delivers the goods and asks no subscription. Therefore one never hears of a party's asking for a guarantee in contracting with the Devil. This is absolute proof that he keeps his contracts steadfastly. It will perhaps be objected that the candor which the Devil shows in pacts and contracts is not to be ascribed to honesty but to selfishness, since he thereby furthers his own business and entices others to contract with him —but are our so-called honest merchants honest in trade solely for the sake of being honest? Does not the sincerity which they show arise from the same source? As the saying goes, when two do a thing it is not necessarily the same thing; what is called virtue in a merchant is called vice in the Devil. Simply because the Devil has a bad reputation, adultery and murder, robbery, thievery, and all evil deeds are ascribed to his influence. I would not go so far as to declare him innocent, although I dare say that the usual accusation which is made against the Devil has a bad effect and is ill-founded. It has a bad effect because sinners avoid accepting guilt and use the Devil as a cloak for their misdeeds. This is inadmissible, for man's depraved flesh and blood can drive him to sin without anyone's co-operation. The Devil is said once to have met a girl in the marketplace who had been seduced and was very obviously with child. He approached her and said, "What is this, my dear Martha? It would seem that you have committed a folly." The girl answered with a sigh, "Needs must when the Devil drives." The Devil, who was quite innocent, grew angry, gave her a box on the ear and said, "Take that, you liar; your own weak flesh is at fault; neither my mother nor I have had the slightest part in your behavior."

The Devil is said also to haunt people at night. The ideas one should entertain about a crafty and evil spirit made me of a different opinion than the learned in this matter, in part since I found such action unreasonable unless one assume the Devil to be in his second childhood (which no one will admit), and in part since by such haunting he would act contrary to his own interests. Because I have been criticized for this opinion I have abandoned it and now admit with the orthodox that it really is the Devil who nocturnally haunts cemeteries, houses, and nurseries. It nevertheless follows that people become more God-fearing, that by such haunting the Devil shows himself to be a friend rather than an enemy of the human race, and that this action therefore should win praise rather than condemnation. His office as the tormentor and executioner of the damned should cast no slur on his name or reputation, for such an office is a necessity. Just as a city cannot do without an executioner, the human race cannot do without such a provost who executes the sentences passed on the guilty. The office in itself is not only necessary but honorable; the ancient Greeks did not hesitate to make two worthy men, Minos and Rhadamanthus, executioners in Pluto's realm.

All this demonstrates that the Devil is not as black as he is painted and, to the contrary, that he has many good qualities. It is therefore less difficult to write a defense for him than for many persons whose actions cannot be excused. Many impartial men have perhaps noted that judgments against the Devil have been too severe; and it might well be that if the learned and impartial theologian Gottfried Arnold, who defended many disliked persons, had lived somewhat longer, he would also have undertaken to write an apology for this notorious spirit. That would not have been so difficult, for as we see, with the help of good rhetoric, things can at least acquire some semblance of truth. It can be said for sure that many who mock the Devil and particularly those who portray him with horns, should watch their tongues, for he can return their raillery and ask them to feel their own foreheads. What is more, it can be reckoned among the Devil's good qualities that he wears his horns with more patience than most men who degrade themselves with lawsuits and summonses. There has never been mention of the Devil's having called any one to court for almost 6,000 years now, so that even if he is a cuckold, he is withal a sensible cuckold who is able to conceal his shame better than human beings. There can be no doubt that the Devil tempts men, but since experience shows that the so-called temptations of the Devil can be counteracted by powders and medicines, it is obvious that the accusation is often ill-founded, unless one assume that devils can be expelled with crab's-eyes or laxatives—and to assume this is to underestimate the enemy.

There you have an apology for the Devil, written in a hurry. From it you may conclude what an able disputer could do if he would agree to defend the case from the cathedra or what an attorney who has the reputation of being able to make black into white might accomplish. Logic and rhetoric are two principal branches of learning. It was with the help of logic that Zeno of Elea demonstrated that nothing in the world moves and that Erasmus Montanus clearly showed that Peer the Deacon was a rooster and that it was meritorious to beat one's parents. Now to speak seriously: I would request that you show this letter to no one, particularly not to Pastor Niels or to Peer the Deacon. They might take everything literally and employ my words as a text for sermons, and I might have the same fate as a certain man who had been a cardinal in the facetious papal college which was founded in this city some years ago. When, after his death, some letters were found addressing him as Cardinal Orsini, the executors took the address literally and conferred with the civil authorities whether the deceased could be buried in hallowed ground.

Purism in Language

Epistle 64

I thank you for your latest communication, but since it contained nothing but foolishness, I shall this time write nothing but foolishness to you.—Last week I had a visitor, a Dutchman. This gentleman claimed to have read my *Moral Thoughts* in German and said that the book had pleased him. But he took offense at the judgment which I had passed upon Dutch purists, i.e., writers who are trying to remove from the language words borrowed from other tongues. I felt that my opinion was not ill-founded, since the labors of these selfsame purists serve only to make the language difficult not only for foreigners but even for the country's own inhabitants. I pointed out to him that a number of his own countrymen, among others the renowned jurist Antonius Matthaeus, had made sport of purism and had charged the linguistic reformers with removing foreign words which have long been in use and which are understood by all, even by common people and peasants, and with introducing in their stead newly fabricated Dutch words comprehensible to no one or with employing long paraphrases and circumlocutions to describe something which can be expressed in a single word. Since the word "pensioners" is of foreign origin, for example, some have felt it better to write *"Loon trekkende Raadsheer,"* in the conviction that they were doing the language a service by making one comprehensible word into three incomprehensible words. He replied to this that one might well permit jurists, philosophers, and artists to employ foreign words of which the language at times may stand in need, and that without reprehension one may borrow vocables from those places where the arts were discovered and where they first acquired their special vocabularies. He said that in other spheres one would do well not to employ foreign words, especially where they are not necessary, for to do so is only to be contemptuous of the language of one's forefathers and to reproach it for its poverty. I expostulated with all the arguments which I adduce in the above-mentioned work, but since I noticed that he was not convinced by them, I finally said, "Sir, do not boast so much of the richness of your language even in everyday matters. If you carry your reformation too far, you can sever your fatherland from its best and only products, *Boter* and

Kaes, which are from the Latin words *butyrum* and *caseus;* yes, you can even lose your tobacco, so that you will have almost nothing left except the heavy and unhealthy air in which you live." When he heard this, he went away silently, as if he had been quite converted, so that I believe I this time made a proselyte with *Boter* and *Kaes.* We may conclude that one who understands the art of catechizing can with humble arguments accomplish more than with the loftiest eloquence and that with *Boter* and *Kaes* one can force a Dutchman to profess the truth.

Foreign Criticism of My Comedies

Epistle 66

I THANK YOU for sending me the foreign criticism of my comedies. I have previously seen other criticism of the same kind, but I do not let it influence me, although I am ordinarily very willing to improve my works, as I presumably have demonstrated in the same comedies, where, as some will remember, I made various changes, until the comedies acquired the form they now possess. Foreign critics speak favorably of my dramas, but some note two mistakes in them: first, that the characters are often exaggerated; second, that *unitas loci & temporis,* that is to say the rules which are established about time and place, are not always respected. With regard to the first, I readily admit that the characters are exaggerated in certain places; but it must be said that the exaggeration is quite intentional and absolutely necessary; for I, as well as others, have learned by observation that dramas without exaggerated characters—i.e., without the very element which academic critics look upon as a mistake—have no effect. If, for example, one describes a miser as starving himself, the character will be quite conventional, and the effect will be that the spectators will either yawn or fall asleep in the theater. What can be more exaggerated than the description which Plautus gives of Euclio—to wit, that when he went to bed he tied a bag around his mouth so that his soul would not leave him and get lost. Yet whatever has amused an audience more than this same exaggerated description? In all my dramas no character is more exaggerated than Jacob von Tyboe's; but he is in every respect no more eccentric than Terence's Thraso or Plautus' *Miles gloriosus,* i.e., the bragging warrior, and nevertheless these pieces are considered to be their respective authors' best comedies. One can here apply what Pliny says about certain conventional writers: *peccant, quia nihil peccant.* The same observations which are now made about my comedies were also made in Molière's time; but that great comedian was not influenced by such criticism, for he had learned by experience that the rules which he was admonished to obey served but to destroy his comedies completely. I speak here from the same experience, for I have been present when my comedies were played in the theater and have there learned that what academic critics censure is the very soul of comedy. I admit that it is a necessity to respect the unities of time and place; I wrote the drama *Ulysses* in order to demonstrate the errors which are perpetrated in works which do not observe those unities; but a good writer of comedy must not make himself such a slave of rules that he rejects a capital story or the most fitting subject for a drama. There are certain subjects which make the best and most pleasing comedies, but which at the same time are of such a nature that the unities of time and place cannot always be respected. For example, the comedy about the transformed peasant, and some others which have been received with the greatest delight by spectators, are of such a nature. Besides, insofar as the subject has permitted, I have carefully observed such rules, yes, at times more carefully than any other writer of comedy. And I venture to say that the play entitled *Henrik og Pernille* can serve as norm which comedies may follow. For in the entire piece are not only all rules carefully observed, but not a single person appears on the stage save at the time and at the very moment he is expected—something to which few writers of comedy have paid attention. Not every subject permits this; but a comedy must nevertheless be a good comedy. Many a drama does not deserve the name of drama, although all logical rules have been respected. Various writers of comedy nevertheless presume that the art of writing comedy consists in following rules and therefore as evidence print on the title-page words like these: "The scene is a room or a nursery and the play lasts four to six hours." If this is the criterion of a good drama, then every schoolmaster can become a writer of comedy; but experience shows that among innumerable writers there are found but few who have produced comedies which meet with any general approbation. I say with any general approbation. The French may speak as fervently as they will about their contemporary writers of comedy; their encomia serve only to show the nation's depraved taste. I do not believe that any connoisseur reads their new dramas save to better his knowledge of the French language. The dramas are almost all dry and confused, so that one might take them to be empty and ostentatious conversations, if their authors did not signify by divisions into acts and scenes that they were meant to be comedies. Molière would not judge differently if he arose from the dead. To write such dramas is any and every man's work, for they do nothing but tell in an elegant way what was said in a certain place for four or six hours. One has only to read the reflections of Lamotte and others about comedies to be convinced how ill-founded modern criticism is. What I write here is not meant to refute my critics, but rather to instruct. I have no reason to complain of their judgments in general, since they bestow upon me greater honor than I might have imagined myself worthy of receiving. Not without pleasure have I read that foreigners have considered an ornament to the nation the comedies which some of my own countrymen have looked upon as unseemly prating.

of Ludvig Holberg

The Tar Water Cure

Epistle 71

In his last missive Milord wants to know my opinion of the tar water cure, and asks whether I would advise him to take the same. I cannot advise against any sort of medicine which large numbers of patients find beneficial. If the inmates of an entire hospital had been cured by the use of phosphorus matches or meat skewers, I could and should do nothing but recommend such remedies. It makes no difference how one is cured, if one is but cured. It is to my mind uncertain whether the patients should ascribe the good results to the efficacy of tar water or to their own strong faith and imagination. It is certain only that innumerable people witness that they have been cured by it and, since that is the case, no one should decry this medicine which, as I hear daily, helps all the weaknesses of the body as well as the mind. I therefore advise Milord and all others to use this water as long as the prescription is credible and in good repute. It is time enough to cease when one notices that this *à la mode* medicine no longer has any effect. I say this *à la mode* drink, since I am not certain how long the imagination will co-operate with the water. If I had as strong faith (or at least a goodly dose of it) as the majority of my fellow citizens, I would long ago have let myself be tarrified, but since I have often experienced that, because of my feeble faith, I have not been able to profit from certain things the way others do, I have not yet wanted to swim with the tide. I do not deny the effectiveness and usefulness of tar, but hitherto I have employed it only to lubricate my wagon, since I not only believe but know that this cure is sure.

I state that, because of my weak faith, I have not been influenced by many things which are very effective for others. I remember having been in company several years ago, for example, where attempts were made to use a divining rod; it turned in everyone's hands except in mine. I could list numerous other things which would corroborate what I say here. I do not disdain medicine, not even the tar water drink; on the contrary, I advise all to use it who can be healed or imagine themselves to be healed by it. I might also try tar water if its flavor were not so loathsome, but since drinking this water can be considered a penance because of its distastefulness and I, for the above-mentioned reasons, cannot be certain of any effect, I prefer to drink tea or coffee, about which it can be said that, even if they are not useful, they are at least not distasteful. Time will tell whether the tar water cure is a reality and whether it is the tar or the imagination which has such good effects. I could list several things which for a time were looked upon as medicinal but since have come to be despised. I prophesy that as soon as some one or other finds himself made worse by tar water it will lose its reputation as well. When coffee was introduced it had an admirable effect; it was reputed to be able to cure everything, including the toothache, but now it is considered by many to be a harmful drink. The reason for this discredit I imagine to be the following: A corseted maiden once had a fainting spell at a coffee table. The real reason may well have been that she was too tightly corseted, but since she imagined that the blame was to be found in the drink rather than in the corset and since her imagination then furnished her with another time in the past when she was similarly affected while uncorseted, her anxiety at once overcame others, so that every other female now looks upon coffee as poison.

The Danish Character

Epistle 72

In my work *A Description of Denmark and Norway,* I portrayed the Danes as a people not given to extremes and in everything following a middle path. The sketch was considered to be accurate at the time, for the people actually had that quality, but if the work were to be republished, I should be obliged to add in a note below the text that the era of moderation had passed and that the nation changed radically some twenty or thirty years ago. Its character more and more resembles the English, so that year by year it has not only a greater propensity but also inclination toward excess and delight in the same. The Danes have sometimes been given to extreme indolence, at other times to extreme activity, at times to timidity, at times to charlatanry. Recently they were censured because of their slothfulness in writing books; now one makes fun of them because of their overindulgence in this respect. Twenty years ago the whole city took to dancing, so that musicians, of which there was suddenly a great lack, had to be imported into the country. Thereupon almost the entire city became musically inclined, but no one wanted to dance. At one time the inhabitants have been as frolicsome as calves, at another as demure and sober as old cats. As far as studies are concerned, one notes particularly strange phenomena: first one subject has been in favor and then another, and always to excess. Some years ago the study of physics was, next to theology, the most popular in our university. Most of the disputes which occurred among students had to do with physical matters. Now, on the other hand, this subject has been pushed aside and forgotten. In the interim the study of Hebrew became the fashion and was cultivated with such ardor that every other student was capable of conducting a synagogue. After the Hebrew era, first one and then another study was carried to excess. For a time our students were smitten with a strange disease, symptoms of which consisted in compiling indices of laws. I call it a disease and am able to look upon it only as the effect of something in the air, since no one can comprehend what motivation there could have been to compile such a quantity of indices at one time, for there already were more than enough of them. After this disease had run its course, the city was teeming with *Spectators* and in such quantities that people were amazed. Since this affectation followed hard upon the last large comet, many imagined it to be a result of that celestial phenomenon. Whereas abroad every nation could account for one *Spectator,* here there arose one in every quarter of the city so that there finally seemed to be as many *Spectators* as watchmen. Fortunately for mankind, which had to withstand a multiple attack, the various *Spectators* declared war upon one another and this diminished their influence and led to a general truce. One sees from this example that the nation's character no longer is the same as it once was and that blood circulates differently in our veins now. The national character has exchanged its stability for volatility, and Danes go from one extreme to the other. Whereas formerly there was but one tone and one heard nothing but *da capo,* now the word is *verte subito.* All this I have not mentioned in order to jest with the nation; I cannot explain such a change as for the worse or the better. I write only to point out that the characterization which I once made is in need of correction, since the nation has now become not only English but arch-English and its ancient motto *semper eadem* no longer is appropriate in our times. There is however one tendency in which the nation has persisted in this period of volatility—to wit, appetite for rank or the so-called *honnête ambition.* This seems more and more to be becoming the object of the Danes' attentive consideration.

Quislimiri

Epistle 79

In answering Milord's last communication, in which he speaks of the inequality of wages, I must say that there are many things which seem to be ill-founded and to be in need of reform which nevertheless upon closer examination are found to be equitable and of such a nature that they should not be altered. There is considerable information on this matter in *Niels Klim's Journey to the World Underground;* indeed it is the foremost concern of the book. The wandering Klim everywhere condemns the subterranean people's customs and conventions, which after careful consideration he finds to be necessary and profound; likewise, he first admires things which he later finds not to be well-founded. Among the conditions which are berated daily and which seem to be quite unreasonable is that offices equal in responsibilities and demanding equal work are so differently remunerated. The criticism is made: what can be more unjust than that A., who holds the same office and has the same and sometimes more work than B., receives only half or perhaps only one-third as much in wages? No complaint can appear better founded, and it is for this reason that various persons have endeavored to establish the equality of wages and salaries for like offices. But these good people would upon closer examination find that this is a sleeping dog it does not pay to waken and that introducing the equality of wages would not have the beneficial effect which they imagine. In support of my point I shall cite an episode which by mistake was not included in Klim's journey and which can serve as a supplement if the book is republished a third time. Klim came to a country called Quislimiri, which was famous on account of its just laws. He found this to be the case: everything was based upon equity; but for all that, he noted to his great amazement that he nowhere had found greater ignorance and indolence. He asked his host, who was a sensible man, what the reason for this could be, and he was told that the people previously were second to no nation in knowledge and celerity but that a law which in itself seemed reasonable had occasioned ignorance and indolence. In conformity with this law all those who had equal work and the same office were to receive equal pay. No law, he said, received more approbation at first, but it was noticed in the course of time that the law had a bad effect. The most numerous offices in this country were those of tumbos and quambos (who corresponded to our priests and sheriffs), and it was to these offices that the common man usually aspired. They were previously remunerated unequally. One tumbo could earn six hundred dollars annually and another who had the very same duties and at times more might receive only two hundred. There was heard considerable complaint about this inequality; for this reason the government found it wise to put all these offices on an equal footing. With the abolition of this inequality all emulation likewise disappeared, so that they who previously had tried to distinguish themselves by their learning and diligence in order to enjoy those posts which were most highly paid, became half-hearted in their studies, and, when someone reproached them, they answered, "Of what use is it that we distinguish ourselves when the wages are the same?" And there was something to what they said. One may rest assured that such an arrangement would everywhere have the same bad effect as in the above-mentioned country. Many things seem to be advantageous and are nevertheless detrimental, and similarly many things bear the appearance of an injustice and nevertheless are based upon reasonableness. I recall that I once was asked whether I was good to my peasants, to which I replied, "Yes, and in particular to those who are well-to-do." This answer seemed evil and unjust, since the general opinion is that one should be kindest to the poor. My answer is based on the fact that, since peasants ordinarily do not inherit anything and since that which they possess has been acquired through their own diligence and skill, a well-to-do peasant is, generally speaking, an industrious and efficient householder, just as a poor peasant generally is an indolent and negligent husbandman. Since this is the case, my answer can signify nothing but that I am kinder to industrious than negligent peasants and that I take care not to lay a greater burden upon a wealthy than upon a poor peasant. Most people who hold to the other view, believing that one should lay the greatest burden upon him who best can bear up under it, have to a certain degree a false and pernicious principle, for the poor are only encouraged in their indolence while the wealthy lose their desire to work, when they note that work is only detrimental to them. Nevertheless, many people do not comprehend this; one observes that they believe it to be a sort of execution of justice to apportion burdens and work in direct relation to their subordinates' well-being, without considering the reason for their subordinates' greater or lesser means, and without realizing the evil consequences which come from such action—to wit, that a diligent and efficient man curses his own industry for which he is punished, as it were, and is irked that, after having drudged and labored while his neighbor drank and slept, he must bear his neighbor's burden. Such does not serve the preservation of society, and it follows therefore that they who hold to such a principle are unfitted to govern either large or small households. On the other hand, circumstances must be taken into consideration here as well as in all other matters, for many a man through no fault of his own, by accident and unfortunate happenings alone, has become poorer than his fellow citizens. To lighten such a man's burden is reasonable and can offend no one, but helping the indolent only arouses resentment and has the effects which have been outlined above.

Depraved Taste in Love

Epistle 89

You express your amazement that such an attractive maiden as N. N. could have fallen in love with M. M. and married a person of such evil qualities about whom one can say nothing more than that he is one of the greatest tobacco smokers in the country. I, on the other hand, am not amazed at this; that can be the very reason that she has fallen in love with him. It happens that many people find smoked meat more to their taste than the fresh. Similarly, many love that for which others have an aversion. In this connection I shall cite two remarkable examples, one from ancient and the other from modern history. A distinguished young woman named Hipparchia became so enamoured of the Cynic philosopher Crates, that she preferred him to all her handsome, distinguished, and wealthy suitors. Indeed, her passion was so great, that she announced to her parents that she would commit suicide if she were not permitted to have Crates as her mate. Her parents requested Crates to dissuade her from such a design, and this he tried to do. His admonition being in vain, he showed her his rags and his wretchedness, saying that she would have to reconcile herself to such slovenliness and such a miserable existence if she would be his wife. Hipparchia did not hesitate for a moment, but dressed herself in a Cynic's rags and wandered everywhere as a beggar with Crates, following his way of life in everything and not hesitating publicly to practice all the improprieties of the Cynic philosophy and to suffer all the scorn and contempt to which its adherents were subjected. The other example from our own time is that of a noble lady who had an unsurmountable antipathy toward her first husband, even though among all the subjects in the kingdom, he was the most distinguished and at the same time the most gallant lord. After she was divorced she entered into another marriage which also had an unhappy end, whereupon she took a common sailor as her third husband. Although he treated her badly every day, she said she was far happier than in her first marriage. This I heard from her own lips, for I was in her house, which was located at a ferry on the island of Falster, when her husband was under arrest because of a misdeed. It would therefore seem that the very thing which was abominable to others was cause for love and pleasure for her. I could cite numerous other examples of such depraved taste, but I shall let these two suffice. I am therefore not amazed when I hear mention of strange marriages. It is with them as with food and drink, where one person finds pleasure in the very thing which is repulsive to most. Because of difference in taste, every maiden finds a husband, every dish finds its gourmet, and every book finds its reader.

of Ludvig Holberg

Tea, Coffee, and Tobacco

Epistle 91

You chide me for drinking tea and coffee which you consider to be detrimental to my health and to weaken my stomach. I am however of a different opinion, particularly with regard to coffee, which I imagine to alleviate all illnesses, so that I use it even for a toothache. This cure will probably seem ridiculous to you, but I speak from experience and can also explain the nature of its palliative effect. My toothache is generally caused by hot and acrid vapors which arise from the stomach and irritate both teeth and brain. Coffee strengthens the stomach, hinders the vapors in rising, and consequently allays both toothache and headache. I have so often experienced this that I have become quite convinced of it. Even if tea and coffee were of no other value, the fact would remain that drunkenness, which previously was so prevalent, has become less common because of their use. Now our wives and daughters pay ten calls in one afternoon and return home quite sober. This was not possible in the old days when there was nothing to offer visitors but Goldwasser, dry wine, Spanish bitters, spiced wine, and the like, of which a lady had at least to take a sip at each place. When all these small doses which were taken in every lying-in-room were added together, the amount could be considerable. If nothing else, ladies then acquired a taste for certain heavy liqueurs with which they now have no acquaintance and for which they therefore can acquire no taste. What one does not know one cannot use; and one cannot desire something until it has been tasted.

You want also to know how long tea and coffee have been in use among Europeans and request the history of these two commodities. Coffee beans, called by the Turks *cahueh* or *caoua,* grow on trees of that name in Arabia. They are also called Levantine beans. Coffee beans are beginning to be imported from India too, but these are not nearly as good as the Levantine beans. The use of coffee beans in most places in Europe can be traced to the end of the seventeenth century. Here in Scandinavia they were introduced later; in my childhood I never heard them spoken of. At first many made use of burned barley which was served as coffee in tea rooms, for people could not yet tell the difference. It is said that the virtue of coffee beans was first noted by a monk to whom a herdsman, who watched over goats and camels in a locality where the beans grew, reported that, when his creatures ate the beans, they stayed awake and were restless the whole night. Thereupon the monk, who was a prior, introduced the use of the beans in the monastery in order to prevent the brothers from sleeping at matins. There is considerable dissension about these beans; some ascribe to them great virtue while others consider them to be harmful. Among the latter is our renowned physician Simon Paulli, who declaimed against them in his commentary on tea and tobacco. Tea has been known in Europe longer, although not prior to the beginning of the previous century. I find that Olearius and Mandelslo speak of it in the accounts of their travels as a hitherto unknown herb, the virtue of which is praised. Like coffee, tea has its enemies, as can be seen by the medical dissertation *De tribus impostoribus thee cafe & chocolade.* Tobacco, which the Americans call *petun* and against which the above-named Simon Paulli also declaims, became first known to Spaniards in the American province of Yucatan. It was presented to the Grand Prior in France and to Queen Catherine de' Medici by the French ambassador Jean Nicot. For this reason it received the name of the nicotine herb and is in Latin still called *herba nicotiana.* For a time it was also called *herbe au grand prieur* or *herbe à la reine.* The herb has had various adversaries besides Simon Paulli. I have in my history of the Persian king Shah Abbas told of the facetious means which he employed in order to wean his subjects from tobacco. King James I of England wrote a tract against tobacco, and Pope Urban VIII published a bull which excommunicated those who use tobacco in church—which can only be understood to mean snuff. It was previously imported only from India; now tobacco is grown in various places in Europe, for it is in great demand. It is not only smoked and used as snuff but in certain places even chewed, particularly by Norwegian peasants who find that it has a heavenly flavor. Others praise this herb's virtue and advantages. We have in Danish a poem in praise of tobacco, which is a masterpiece of Danish poetry. Quarreling with no one's taste, I for my part can neither praise nor censure those who find pleasure in it. Whether the use of tobacco has the good effect which some claim, I cannot say. It must be admitted that smoking is no natural pleasure; rooms are dirtied and clothing spoiled by it, not to mention the many accidents and fires caused by pipe smoking. For the last-named reason it is generally stipulated in the rules for tenant farmers and bailiffs that no one on a farm may smoke tobacco, but the rule is seldom kept. The desire for tobacco has so enslaved most persons that neither punishment nor threats can keep them from it. Nowhere is there greater misuse of tobacco than in Holland, as one notices especially in traveling on barges. One scarcely hears a pipe being blown clean before the flint and steel are struck again. There is also great overindulgence in snuff, so that some persons have as many snuffboxes as pockets and one scarcely sees them put one box away before they reach into a different pocket for another. I have used snuff to excess myself but have for some time sought to be more moderate in its use as in everything else, even in the use of the coffee that you warn me against. I generally take no more than four to five cups a day.

Does Witchcraft Exist?

Epistle 92

Milord's enquiry about witchcraft I can answer only in the same way as his enquiry about ghosts—to wit, that there are told so many credible tales that it is difficult to deny witchcraft entirely. On the other hand, there are related so many unreasonable fables that one has good reason to believe nothing. That which undermines belief in witchcraft most is the fact that the more one doubts its reality, the more it diminishes. What increases daily in the face of firm belief diminishes daily in the face of unbelief, so that doubt has effected more than the most severe punishment and the strictest laws. In olden days, when the authorities hunted out witches and wizards and punished them by burning at the stake, every other matron was in some places said to ride a broomstick to Blocksberg or Hecla, and pacts were found which had been made with the Devil. At the time of James I and Charles II there was much witch hunting, and England was full of witches. During the reign of Henry IV more than six hundred suspects were burned while the parlement was at Bordeaux; but when the punishment ceased to be meted out, the art of necromancy slowly disappeared. Around Paris one hears almost nothing about necromancy, since the parlement does not pass judgment on such matters. A Cornelius Loos, a Bekker, and others have with their publications divorced the Devil from his old means of sustenance in Holland. Indeed, the Devil's business in this part of the world has so diminished in the course of time that it is now limited practically to the Finnmark, where it flourished until the end of the last century, as long as the local governors and judges continued to subscribe to the country's old orthodox beliefs. The first man to cut a clean swath was Governor Lork. I can give an example of this man's heterodoxy from my own years in Bergen. Once when he visited a judge and saw a Lapp lying stretched out upon the floor, he was puzzled. When he asked what this signified, the judge said, "Quiet, *mon frère,* his soul has departed from his body and when it returns we shall hear some news." The governor then said, "It will perhaps take too long. I shall bring the soul back at once," whereupon he took his cane and gave the Lapp such a blow on the rump that he jumped up with a great roar. One observes from this how different the governor was from his predecessors and that he might well have been a man of justice but have been detrimental to the Lappland trade, for the Devil could not prosper as long as such a governor was in office—and from this time on there was a marked decrease in the trade. This incident serves to strengthen the view that witchcraft and the black art find their greatest support in the superstitions and credulity of government officials, unless one would believe either that the Devil has become less active in his old age or that he has lapsed into a state of insolvency and that, because of financial embarrassment, he no longer can support as many necromancers as before and that people will not bind themselves by pacts any more, since they note that he is not in a position to make the usual advance of money and can for his part no longer *praestere praestanda*. In my youth I once found a document in which a young man had bound himself to the Devil and stipulated an annual payment of a barrel of gold. I delivered the document to the young man's tutor, who tore it to pieces and bade me be silent about the matter, saying that he would punish the young man privately. One might deduce from this that the Devil was not in a position to pay such a sum and therefore had not wanted to take on the obligation; but such opinions find no approbation. It is credible that most of what is related about witchcraft is based upon fable or pure illusion and therefore that Bekker's *Betoverde Weereld* might be considered a useful work, had the author not gone too far and explained everything that is told about spirits as fables and figments of the imagination. He who neither rejects nor accepts all tales proceeds more judiciously. Most people are unable to stop in their reforms, however, and as soon as they discover that they have been deceived once, they ascribe everything to deception. How this can happen and does happen every day I have demonstrated in my play *Neither Head nor Tail*. In it is shown how a person can pass from unbelief to superstition and again from superstition to unbelief, so that when he does not respect certain rules prescribed in the comedy and does not keep matters under control, as it were, in examining a thing, he falls from one extreme into the other, so that he first believes too much, then too little; first everything, then nothing.

Women's Society as Recreation

Epistle 99

You express wonder that although I am growing old and always have been devoted to study, I find more pleasure in the society of women than of men. You will wonder even more when I say that it is for the sake of my studies that I seek such company. In order to understand this paradox you should know that when I am at home I am always engaged in work which racks my brain and that I go out solely for the sake of the recreation which my mind needs. Such recreation is to be found above all in ladies' chambers, where there generally is heard nothing but everyday conversation which requires no meditation. When I have acquired a headache by studying, there is therefore no one I would rather visit than Madame N. N., who tells me nothing except the food she has eaten that day, or how many eggs her chickens laid that week, or similar subjects that put no strain on the mind or the sinews of the brain. In the company of men, on the other hand, there arise discussions which make me rack my brain. They speak of lawsuits and affairs of state, subjects which can be useful and even agreeable at certain times, but not when one is in company in order to refresh the mind and to rest the brain. As soon as the first greeting has been spoken, someone starts to explain (and then to ask my opinion) about a lawsuit in which judgment has been passed that very day in the town hall or the supreme court, or someone else involves me in questions of state occasioned by a new ordinance or the latest newspaper. This is like suggesting a game of chess to a person who comes tired from his desk and therewith making him cogitate once more. In this connection Englishmen give evidence of their powers of discernment, for they dislike games which require concentration. Their backgammon, for example, is not nearly so complex as our trick-track. The same can be said of other games: cock fighting, bull-fighting and such like. *Le jeu d'echecs,* say the French, *n'est pas assez jeu.* That is, chess and similar games are not games but a study in themselves. They are for the idle who fear that their brains will grow rusty, but not for industrious folk who seek recreation in games and in the society of others. It is for this reason that businessmen have set certain hours of the day when they want to hear nothing but harmless conversation. It is said that Richelieu kept such harmless company an hour a day, for he could not find the recreation he sought by entering into a metaphysical discussion when he came tired from his cabinet. It was for the same reason that Socrates occasionally romped with his children. Another reason I prefer the company of women is that whenever I come together with men I am given either a glass of wine or a pipe of tobacco, which is not at all to my taste. When with ladies, on the other hand, I get tea, coffee, and gossip, and this suits me best in my idle hours. There you have the reason for my mode of life.

Compliments

Epistle 109

On my journeys abroad I have noticed that the farther south one proceeds, the less food and the more compliments one receives. This is not to the taste of Northern peoples, who would prefer to have one course more and one compliment or courteous expression less. It is therefore that one of our courtiers who traveled with the late King Frederik IV in Italy always ordered food for four persons in hostelries although he was alone. Compliments increase as one advances toward the equator and accounts for fewer degrees of latitude, until they at last become quite ridiculous and absurd. Here in the North we let it suffice to greet one another with "your servant," a greeting which our peasants, who say only "God's peace" and "Good-day," think to be rather affected. In France this greeting does not suffice, for there one says, "I have the honor to be your servant." In Italy one goes still farther, for there even one peasant says to the other, "I am the slave of your lordship" *(Schiavo di vossignoria),* and in Spain one compliments even beggars to whom one does not wish to give alms. Instead of using the Northern expression "nothing for you this time" or the French refusal *"Dieu vous bénisse,"* which is somewhat finer although it does not satisfy the stomach any better, Spaniards dismiss a beggar with profuse compliments attesting that they are sorry they cannot help him and asking that their action not arouse resentment. In the Orient and above all in China the *façons de parler* are the most splendid and the compliments the most exaggerated, so that it is looked upon as coarseness to express oneself naturally. Everything there is a formality; one person compliments the other for half an hour before passing through a door; everything happens in cadence, so that at a banquet the guests eat in rhythm. Several travelers have described Oriental courtesies which cannot be seen or heard by Europeans without their provoking mirth. In Persia, for example, it is impolite to say to anyone that a person is dead; instead the following expression is employed: He has given you the rest of the time in which he might have lived. Chardin relates that this compliment was once misused and occasioned laughter. Shah Abbas II had given an officer custody of a horse, which died in his care. When the king asked about the horse, the officer replied, "It has given Your Majesty the rest of the time it might have lived," at which the king had to laugh, saying, "My thanks to you for wanting to add a horse's age to mine." This recalls a condolence which once was expressed here when a person, instead of saying, "I am sorry your father is dead," said, in order to put it more elegantly, "I am sorry that your dear father arrived in heaven too suddenly," to which the mourning son replied, "Thank you for your condolence, and I hope that your dear father may not come there so suddenly." I for my part find nothing more repugnant than exaggerated speech and an unnatural way of life; consequently I generally excuse myself when I am invited to a dinner here, and I could not submit to a Chinese banquet unless I were sentenced to it by a court.

Authors and Their Public

Epistle 112

Observing the meager fruits which generally are harvested by writing, one can but wonder why there are so many writers. I shall not speak of the annoyance to which writers are subjected—such as envy when they write well and derision when they write poorly. No works are attacked more vehemently than those which are written with the greatest care. This I can prove by my own as well as others' examples. With regard to Latin style I have never received more compliments than for my third Latin epistle, but since my style has never been censured more by learned journals than it has in that selfsame epistle, I conclude that a journalist undertook to criticize the style simply because he heard it generally praised. He who writes something which is mediocre and commonplace avoids altercations but subjects himself to contempt. That is the fate of most writers, and not without reason, for most of them write simply to write—that is, to express in a different way that which has been written a hundred times before. The learned Huetius maintains therefore that all which has been written since the beginning of the world could be put into nine or ten folios, had it been said but once. He excepts histories, but the many volumes of history could also be reduced to few if everything regurgitated were eliminated. It is, for example, possible to read the history of Alexander the Great in more than a hundred different books, and one universal history is not sold before there appears another in different dress. Such works reap either envy or contempt, but even though an author write a work so that it does not call forth such unpleasantry, it is nevertheless not free from attack, because of readers' varying taste; for that from which one reader derives pleasure disgusts another. A Demosthenes, a Cicero, and a Livy could not write to please everyone. As much as the ancients made of Homer, we see that he nevertheless had many severe critics, even among those who profited most from reading him. On this account a certain author not unfittingly compares these judges with children who strike their nurse from whose milk they acquired their strength. Caligula, who is considered to have been a connoisseur of books, treated Homer with contempt and would have forbidden his being read. When others remonstrated with him he said, "Plato excluded all poets from his Republic; why may I not have the liberty to exclude a single one?" Alcibiades went to the other extreme. Coming one day into a school and failing to find Homer among the schoolbooks, he gave the schoolmaster a box on the ear.

In order to conform to readers' varying taste, certain authors combine wit and earnestness, and lofty with vulgar material, just as a storekeeper has all sorts of wares, one who would give a banquet all sorts of dishes, and musicians various melodies. What one person rejects, another finds to his taste, so that no one departs dissatisfied. One reader wants books which are spirited, while another finds to his taste only books that are erudite, and a third person is disgusted with both sorts. One reader objects to quotations in a book; another looks down upon a book if its margins are not embroidered with them. Some like a concise style, others a voluminous. One wants short, another long sentences. Since this is the case, certain writers have felt it necessary to imitate cooks who make a ragout without any predominant ingredients. Terence is rejected by some because of his dryness, Plautus because of his gaiety, Pliny because of his ornate style, Cicero because of his ornamented style, Horace because of the slackness, and Juvenal because of the severity, of his ethics. In short, no matter how splendid a work is, it finds its detractors unless it is put together after the prescribed fashion. As the saying goes: *toujours chapon:* one tires of monotonous works even though they may be intrinsically excellent. I have noticed, for example, that my plays could have been presented with greater success had they been less animated and had witty sayings been less abundant, for ingenuity is more effective when it is infrequent, just as green fields are more striking to the eye when they are found here and there among mountains and rocks; and the sweetness of honey is not really appreciated unless it is eaten after bitter, sour, or strong foods. Some authors have tried to suit their readers' taste by praising their own works. Cato, Cicero, Scaliger, and other great men have tried to win prestige for their works in this way. Nothing is more common than to find words like these on title-pages: "compiled with great pains," or "a work representing ten or twenty years' labor." Malherbe speaks of his own works thus: *Les ouvrages communs vivent quelques années; Ce que Malherbe écrit, dure éternellement.* Arrianus says of himself that among writers he is the same as Alexander the Great among military heroes, but such self-praise dupes no one except the common man.

Ancient Theories of the Origin of Man

Epistle 121

The ancient philosophers who had no knowledge of God's revealed word formed several strange hypotheses about the origin of man. The most common opinion was that which is found in Diodorus Siculus. He says that when the world still was young there arose in several places on its outer surface or rind mounds and swellings as a result of the sun's warmth. These mounds were refreshed by the dew of the night and invigorated by the warmth of the day until the seed which they contained ripened and grew strong and finally broke out of the mounds. It was by such means that human beings as well as other creatures were supposed to have been created. Each of these creatures immediately sought the most fitting element. The birds took to the air, the fish to water, other creatures established themselves on the earth, and members of each genus united in marriage and were propagated. The earth was thus held to be our mother and the sun our father, for the first living creatures arose from their union in the same way that trees and plants now grow. In order to strengthen this hypothesis there was cited the tale that in Egypt the soil still brings forth a large number of live rats after the Nile has overflowed and made it fertile. Several other philosophers tried to combat this opinion and stated that if such a creation once had taken place it must necessarily occur several times. They were not satisfied with the argument based on the example of certain women who gave birth but once, and on the newness of the earth when it brought forth such seed solely through the effect of the sun. They said further that since experience shows that newly born children cannot live without the help of others, it is incomprehensible that human beings could have kept alive after birth. It was presumed to be sure that these swellings or eggs could, like women's breasts, produce milk and serve to feed the newly born human beings, but since a child needs nourishment for several years and needs help of various kinds before it can fend for itself, this argument can bear no weight. The example of the Egyptian rats may be based upon false reports. A parallel can perhaps be drawn with the various flies, worms, and insects which our forefathers believed to be engendered by evil and filth, but which we now know by experience not to originate in such a way. Since other naturalists have observed that the opinion about the creation of man from the earth is not valid, they have endeavored to establish a different origin—although with little success. I shall pass over the many different opinions in the matter and shall speak only of Anaximander's hypothesis. That philosopher says that since a child needs help of various kinds, the first human beings cannot have been engendered by mire, as claimed, but must rather have been engendered by certain animals who bred with animals of a different genus, and that the combination must have produced offspring of a more perfect kind.

A human being can therefore be an extract or quintessence of several animals who provided the nourishment for the new offspring. From this strange hypothesis it follows that a *politicus* can be engendered by a fox and a snake, a lawyer by a parrot and a magpie, a *grammaticus* by a goat and a ram, a military hero by a lion and a tigress, a seaman by a cod and an oyster, a hunter by a cat and a greyhound, etc.; indeed my *Metamorphosis* or work about the transformation of animals into human beings becomes quite credible or at least just as reliable as Hesiod's *Theogony* or genealogy. Merry-Andrew's opinion of his fickle mistress can also be made credible, for he opined that his mistress was a quintessence or extract of several modest and elusive animals.

Heathen Ethics

Epistle 130

I have myself heard the criticisms of my book *Moral Thoughts* which Milord mentions in his last communication. I am also aware that some have in derision called the book "heathen ethics," but one cannot be offended by people who need rather to be instructed than testily refuted. Moral philosophy is one subject and theology another. If we undertake to write of the former it is necessary to base our doctrines on the teachings of nature; otherwise the subject matter would not correspond to the title. If we write the latter, Christian ethics alone are the basis. Pufendorf, for example, moralized in one way and Buddeus in his *Theologia morali* in another. Both works are praised, since both authors wrote in accordance with the titles of their respective books. Christian ethics are founded on the teachings of nature; the only difference is that Christian ethics are more fully delineated. From this it does not follow that authors are to be looked upon as heathens because they undertake to show man's duty from nature's teachings and because to this end they employ ancient philosophical works and testimony which the Apostles themselves did not despise. It is related that Saint Jerome was whipped by the Devil at night because he read Cicero so zealously, but we observe that most of the church fathers considered reading the works of Seneca and other secular moralists to be useful. A person has but to try reading them in order to be convinced, for there are here and there splendid thoughts about the divine being and profound admonitions regarding man's duty. Seneca says that neither reward nor punishment should force us to practice virtue, for no one is virtuous and righteous save him who loves virtue and righteousness. Plato says that the worship of God does not consist only in sacrifices but in a pure heart and that we should not ask God for anything but what he deems to be for our best. The description which Plato gives of a true virtue in his *Republic* is so noble that one can consider it evangelic doctrine in the mouth of a heathen. He says the righteous man must go forward on the path of virtue even though other men would capture, flay, and crucify him. Epictetus says that if you let it be known that someone has spoken ill of you, you should instead of refuting him reply thus: He who spoke in this way about me must not have known of my other weaknesses, otherwise he would not have failed to mention them too. Marcus Aurelius advises us to love our enemies; and when Diogenes was asked how one could obtain revenge from one's enemies, he said that could be accomplished by bettering one's own life. Epaminondas was once perturbed and when his friends asked the reason, he replied, "I grieve at the vain joy which I yesterday displayed because of the victory at Leuctra." Nothing can be more moving than the resignation to God's will which is shown by Epictetus. His words are these:

As for me, I would fain that death overtake me occupied with nothing but my own moral purpose, trying to make it tranquil, unhampered, unconstrained, free. This is what I wish to be engaged in when death finds me, so that I may be able to say to God, "Have I in any respect transgressed Thy commands? Have I in any respect misused the resources which

Thou gavest me, or used my senses to no purpose, or my preconceptions? Have I ever found any fault with Thee? Have I blamed Thy governance at all? I fell sick, when it was Thy will; so did other men, but I willingly. I became poor, it being Thy will, but with joy. I have held no office, because Thou didst not will it, and I never set my heart upon office. Hast Thou ever seen me for that reason greatly dejected? Have I not ever come before Thee with a radiant countenance, ready for any injunctions or orders Thou mightest give? And now it is Thy will that I leave this festival; I go, I am full of gratitude to Thee that Thou hast deemed me worthy to take part in this festival with Thee, and to see Thy works, and to understand Thy governance."

Can anyone read of such resignation and remain unmoved? It would perhaps seem too extravagant in the mouth of another, but we know that Epictetus' life in every way corresponded to his teachings. If the Devil whips someone who reads this sort of thing, it cannot be at God's command; the Devil must be acting for another reason. Since he does not profit when men become more virtuous, he should keep them from such reading rather than encourage it. Gold is gold wherever it is found, and wisdom is wisdom no matter from whose mouth it flows. The only difference is that words of wisdom from a man whose life corresponds to his words edify more than the wisdom of another who has nothing to recommend him except the honor of being listed on the church rolls, and of having the right to chasten people for that which he himself practices daily. Milord will perhaps answer to all this that heathen ethics cannot be judged on the basis of some few wise heathens' works. The philosophers who pronounced such teachings about God and man's duty are however not so few as might be thought. If their testimony does not suffice, there may be cited certain countries' laws that attest equally sound doctrine. The preface to Zaleukos' ancient law is as follows: Above all, one must believe that a God exists; one has but to cast one's eyes heavenwards and observe the splendor of creation in order to be convinced of it. As a consequence we are obliged to honor the Creator—not only by sacrifices and gifts but by a holy life, in which God finds greater pleasure than in all sacrifices.

On Suicide

Epistle 135

Among the strange and unusual individuals with which the North has not been so richly endowed as other parts of the world was Johannes Robeck, a Swedish author. This same Robeck was born in Kalmar in 1672. He made great progress in scholarly pursuits. While Robeck was continuing his studies in Uppsala, the reflections of the Emperor Marcus Antonius Aurelius fell into his hands and he was overcome by great contempt for the world. Because the university's chancellor, who was perhaps dubious of Robeck's doctrines, would not permit him to dispute publicly in Uppsala, Robeck left his fatherland out of resentment and went to Germany, where he was persuaded by Jesuits into accepting Roman Catholicism. Thereupon he traveled all over Italy. After he had wandered about for a long time, he felt a desire to live in his fatherland again and received permission from King Charles XII to stay there. After the death of the king he, as an apostate and a Jesuit, was no longer permitted to remain in Sweden. As a consequence he left the country a second time and again visited Catholic places. In 1734 he came to Rinteln, where he secluded himself in melancholy for a long time. After having drawn up his testament and sent most of his possessions and work to the learned Funccius, who was staying in the same city, he set out alone in a boat which he had purchased. To everyone's amazement he rowed away from shore. No one knew what this meant, but soon thereafter his corpse was found in the Weser River not far from Bremen, so that no one doubted that he had taken his life out of melancholy; this conviction was strengthened by a work which he had left and which Funccius had been asked to publish. The work is called "A Philosophical Consideration of Suicide." In it the author endeavors to defend the act of suicide; to this end he adduces all the arguments which can support his case. He shows that suicide was respected as a heroic deed among the most moral nations, and he maintains that Lactantius and Augustine were the first who condemned it. He girds himself with what he thinks are twelve principal demonstrations; these are nevertheless easy to refute. The most important seems to be this: A person finds he is incurably ill; he sees no way of being useful in the world; on the contrary, he believes himself only to be a burden to others. He suffers constant pain which tries his patience. How can he be said to sin who under these circumstances shortens a useless life and at the same time brings his suffering to an end? Moralists have hitherto made two replies to this argument: (1) The greater the suffering, the more the patient is to be acclaimed who strives to wait the hour of death set by God and the more edifying his example is to his neighbor. (2) Many diseases which are considered incurable can nevertheless be overcome and terminated through patience and confidence in God. The most reasonable heathens have been of the same mind and have compared men with sentries who are put at certain posts which they must not relinquish. Whatever one may say, it is foolish to want to make suicide into a heroic deed. I concur in the opinion of those who believe it presumptuous to praise and difficult to excuse, although I by no means subscribe to the harsh judgment of the common people and of some ecclesiastics, who would deny persons committing suicide divine bliss and grace. Above all, no doctrine must be professed which detracts from God's justice and mercy and through which a mistaken idea is given of His holy qualities. I rectify my theology accordingly and believe that in so doing my heterodoxy can be excused. How should a ruler be judged who displayed constant wrath and disfavor toward a subject because he did not evince stoic endurance in pain and suffering? To bear up under such temptations is a quality which approaches heroism, and they who have lost their courage in the face of great pain or tribulation should consequently be looked upon as frail and imperfect rather than rebellious subjects who have earned eternal punishment and who have made themselves undeserving of all grace. It is one thing not to be able to excuse a deed and another to dictate eternal punishment for it. Experience teaches us that human beings love life, so we may conclude that they who commit such an act must be overcome by fear, suffering, and tribulation, and indeed must be in a condition which arouses pity rather than wrath. I admit that they who lose courage under such circumstances should not be excused, and I admit also that the authorities do not do wrong in setting an example by refusing to bury them in Christian soil, but I believe nevertheless that they are too harsh in their judgments who think such wretched persons to be unworthy of all grace, especially if the deed was committed in the fallacious belief that it was not sinful. God's judgments will in many things doubtless be different from human judgments. We condemn those who show impatience when they are suffering, but God's holy qualities charge us to temper our judgments. The principle which I here defend also causes me to judge those who die in despair and who consider themselves unworthy of divine grace more leniently than profligate persons who die with the same brazenness and assurance that they displayed during their lives, for the former evince self-contempt, which is a sort of humility and fear of God, whereas the latter exhibit pride and little fear of God—yes, something which approaches atheism.

The Prerequisite of Scientific Explanation

Epistle 141

The dissertation which you have written about the ship that was seen in the moon some years ago is quite learned and indicates the fertility of your mind in finding the most reasonable hypotheses for natural occurrences, but it seems to me that before you undertook to investigate the subject you should have assured yourself of its actual existence, so that your labors would not be wasted. I recall that a man some years ago evolved a theory of the moon. His calculations were presumably correct but were valid only if he could give that celestial body the velocity he wished in order to support his system. Niels Klim's journey gave that sort of person occasion to explain certain phenomena in the subterranean world, but men should first have determined the correctness of the story before racking their brains in trying to establish the causes of such phenomena and before giving reasons for something which does not exist. In this connection, Montaigne remarks, "I generally observe that, when a matter is set before them, men are more ready to waste their time in seeking the reason for it than in seeking the truth of it. They stride over facts, but they diligently investigate consequences. They usually begin thus, 'How can that be explained?' They should say, 'Did it really happen?' "

I recall once disputing in Paris with a zealous Roman Catholic about the infallibility of the pope. He said, "How can it be possible that the popes, as the successors of St. Peter, to whom God gave the promise of infallibility, have been able to err in matters of faith?" To this I replied, "Let us first determine whether the popes are St. Peter's successors in the Roman bishopric and further whether God made such a promise. Thereafter we can decide the other question." Nothing is more perverse than to be absorbed in the investigation of things which are but figments of the imagination, and to search in order to search but not to find.

Democritus once had on his table some figs which tasted of honey. This made him want to see the place where the figs had been gathered. His cook, who observed that he was agitated about it, said laughing that he should spare himself the trouble since she had put the figs into a bowl which had contained honey. Democritus grew angry at this, because the opportunity to investigate a curiosity had been taken from him, and he said, "I shall investigate the cause nevertheless, just as if it were natural." There might be cited innumerable examples to support what I have said here, but I shall let a single one suffice. During the previous century it was rumored that certain persons were to be found in Spain who could see deep into the earth and thereby could recognize metal, water, coffins, and other things. The report agitated naturalists, and several of them tried to determine natural causes for the phenomenon, but none of them troubled themselves to investigate the veracity of the report. These sharp-sighted persons were called Zahoris, an Arabic word which shows that the Moors presumably duped the Spaniards with the tale. When Plutarch once was asked why a foal which had been chased by wolves ran more quickly than others, he replied, "Perhaps because it is not true."

Modern Ironic Moralists

Epistle 157

A certain man into whose hands some of my letters have fallen has reproached me for occasionally having tried to defend errors and vices, and particularly because in one epistle I wrote a defense of the Devil. I note that the gentleman in question takes everything literally without realizing that my defense is pure irony, whereas irony is the most effective means to combat human vices and follies. It is this style of writing which the great master Socrates viewed as the most effective of all to improve men. Among modern moralists, Erasmus of Rotterdam has particularly distinguished himself in this genre. Our century has produced a great master in the Englishman Dr. Swift, for most of his moral writings are full of Socratic ironies. His most recent work, in which he cleverly censures the breeding of youth, has, so I am told, found least approbation in England, but it seems to me nevertheless to be the best of his writings. The author pretends to reprimand those parents who send their children to school to receive instruction in languages and sciences through which neither happiness nor the respect of others can be achieved in these times. On the other hand, the children are not taught more advantageous subjects such as compliments, elegant motions of the body, the movements of the fan, and such like, which grace young people and make them agreeable in company. He says that he therefore has compiled a glossary of several hundred subtleties of which one can employ a certain number every day. There is thus a supply for an entire year, and when the year is past one can begin all over again. He says further that he intends to compile a glossary of *à la mode* oaths but that he has found this to be difficult, since certain oaths which are elegant and proper for a workman or a lackey are improper for a lord. This is roughly the content of his book, from which we deduce that he would banter with us and reprove the education of youth.

A recent author has gone even further. In a publication entitled *Some Thoughts concerning Happiness* he ridicules the Naturalists or so-called freethinkers. The book begins with a letter to a member of Parliament in which the author suggests the abolition of certain old ordinances, generally called the Ten Commandments. He pretends that these ordinances are at variance with the freedom and privileges of the English people and says that several sensible and well-meaning persons have long sought their abolition. He thereupon attacks each commandment in particular and demands that, if the commandments cannot be done away with entirely, they at least be limited by an act of Parliament or expounded in a way other than the way which generally obtains. With regard to the commandment, "Thou shalt not take God's name in vain," he says that it means no more than that one should say or do nothing unless it serves some purpose or advantage. One cannot be said to take God's name in vain if one employs it in order to surprise an opponent or to tease a doubting friend. Keeping the Sabbath, he continues, is only for the common people, or canaille, that is, for those who because of neediness and poverty must work six days a week and can rest only on the seventh day. The commandment lays no obligation on the so-called *honnête* folk who are in a position to eat, drink, and be merry through the year without working. What is more, he says Sunday may not be considered a day of rest in so far as it is coupled with attending church and practicing devotions, for churchgoing is more strenuous than restful for a distinguished person of rank, who finds more rest and pleasure in fresh air in summer and in a warm room in winter than in freezing at church, where he often must listen to unpleasant discourses. The commandments, "Thou shalt not slay" and "Thou shalt not commit adultery," he explains, cannot be taken literally, since they are in contradiction with the conduct of all distinguished persons who know how to live. The phrase "to slay" does not concern those who can boast of sixteen ancestors, especially when it is a common burgher who is killed, for killing such a person is no more deserving of rebuke than the burgher's swallowing a live oyster. It is well-known that this always and everywhere has been looked upon as a *point d'honneur* and that a person of rank must avenge himself, since is improper for such a person and especially for an officer to subject himself to the courts. Adultery is likewise forbidden only for the common people, for it would be ridiculous were workmen to play the parts of *petits maîtres* and to ape persons of rank. Furthermore, adultery requires money and gallant breeding which the common people lack. Therefore this commandment does not bind the wealthy and the distinguished who have enough money to use for such purposes. What is more, we know by experience that the offspring of many common women have been ennobled by such commerce. We see, too, that many a common citizen finds it to his advantage in several respects for his wife to enjoy the acquaintance of wealthy and distinguished persons. *Volenti non fit injuria, etc.* With such irony the author continues to censure the depravity of our times. Although foolish persons can take offense at it, reasonable and discerning minds nevertheless see what the author means by it. I aver that such a judgment should be passed on certain works which I have written in the same style and with the same intent. My defense of the Devil would show only that nothing is so false and unreasonable but that an able writer can gloss it over.

The Punctual Man
Epistle 158

Nothing graces a man more than orderly living, nor does anything preserve human life better. Pliny the Younger cites the examples of several Roman gentlemen who reached a great age and enjoyed enduring good health through orderly living. It would seem that our common friend Metrodorus has undertaken to follow the example of such men. Whether he has been successful in imitating them, Milord must judge from the description below.

Both winter and summer Metrodorus sleeps until precisely three minutes after nine, and as soon as he rises from his bed one can be certain what time it is, more certain than from any clock. Then he rings after his maid, unless it be one of the two days in the week when she shares his bedroom (for he is orderly and has set times in such matters too). As soon as he is in his robe he takes a moderate dose of brandy to open the stomach, as the physicians put it, but this he immediately tempers with tea or coffee, which he uses alternately every other day. Thereupon he sits down in his easy-chair and, after having taken a little morning nap, he spends almost a whole hour reading good books and above all two that he believes cannot be read too often. The one is a devotional work entitled *Revelation's Master Key;* the other is a collection of ordinances pertaining to rank and precedence which he has had bound in one volume; from perusing it daily he is so well versed that he can say within a hair's breadth in which class and under what number every official or person with a degree is to be found. He scarcely concerns himself with any other reading during the forenoon, in the conviction that they who read all sorts of publications learn nothing to their advantage. When the time is precisely thirteen minutes past twelve, he sits down at the table and enjoys a good dinner, although the dinner seldom consists of more than six courses. When the meal is over, he again sits in an easy-chair and picks up a German book called *A True Christian's Nightcap,* in which he reads a passage not so much out of devotion as in order to fall asleep. This is done according to his physician's advice, for the reading of this work has always had the same admirable effect. After he has slept one hour or one and a half hours at the most, his maid comes in with a pipe filled with Canaster tobacco. This he smokes, and while so doing he walks back and forth fifty times, taking a pinch of strong Brazilian snuff every tenth time. Thereafter he drinks brandy from a liqueur glass which holds three fluid ounces. He then has a mental paroxysm or inward penitent struggle and calls the maid.

Mlle. Ignatia comes in trembling, for she knows that the confessional will last an hour. He examines her conduct, reproaches her for her carnality, and exhorts her to lead a new life, which she, with folded hands, always promises to do, although she never keeps her word; that is not his fault, however. After the catechization is over, peace overtures are made and the worthy and compliant girl always shows her docility, so that each tragedy is followed by a little sequel which I nevertheless believe takes place in all sincerity, although his enemies draw their own conclusions about that. They may very well do him an injustice, for those who know the man are of the opinion that he is master of his passions by day and that he does not confound the day's work with night-time affairs. Every task has for him its certain time, so that he does not veer from his strict and measured diet, even in such pleasures. His evening meal which follows is frugal, for he takes one course less than at dinner. When the meal is over, the maid comes in and picks lice from his head until he gets sleepy and wants to go to bed. After undressing him the maid generally goes away, for, as I have noted above, it is only twice a week that she keeps him company at night. In this same way all the days of the week are spent, in fact all the days of the year. Whether such an existence is philosophic, I cannot say, yet everyone must admit that no way of life could be more orderly, since not only the hours but even the minutes are accounted for in everything. To be sure, his critics query how piety can be consistent with brandy, and philippics with love, but numerous sensible moralists witness that there is a sort of piety which is engendered by liquors, for it is said of Cato, *Virtus eius incaluit mero,* and that in love nothing is evil if the heart is but good, and that one cannot sin with the body when the soul is pure. I make no decision in this dispute; I want merely to show that everything about this man is fastidious and elegant and that for this reason he is by some reckoned among the philosophers of our time.

Good and Bad History

Epistle 162

From Milord's last missive I infer that he is not pleased with what I wrote about the uncertainty of history. It does not follow, however, that I deprecate the reading of histories. My remarks show rather a high esteem for history and a solicitousness to cleanse so noble a study of fables and absurdities. I consider that next to God's word, no branch of knowledge is more useful and more important than history when read correctly. From it I learn to know countries; I learn to know people; I learn to know myself. I even learn to prophesy, for on the basis of what has happened in the past, it is possible to conclude what will happen in the future, and therefore I consider every reliable historian in a sense to be a prophet. Moral reflections are doubtless very useful, but history has a more penetrating effect when it is read with discernment and when it is cast in the proper form. Most persons read only for the sake of having something to talk about when in company and are therefore primarily concerned with names and dates or things which tax only the memory. Such readers cannot be said to reach the pith of history; they are satisfied with its bark alone. Similarly they can and should not be called historians who compile dry annals from which we learn nothing except that certain persons were born or died in certain years, that wars were fought, sieges took place, and fortresses were captured. Nevertheless, most writers of history conform to their readers' depraved taste, so that burials, coronations, tournaments, triumphal entries, the capitulation of fortresses, and such like are described in great detail. It is therefore no wonder that histories which could be contained in a few pages take up whole thick folios. In the old Greek and Latin histories and biographies no such padding is found. The ancient historians consider it improper to fill their histories with such useless material as may be found in the works of our contemporaries. In order to be convinced of this, one has but to compare the biographies written by Plutarch, Suetonius, and others with those written nowadays. If Herodotus, Thucydides, or Xenophon had written in the style of the *Theatrum Europæum,* there would have resulted some hundred large volumes instead of three ordinary books. Milord now observes where I am aiming with my criticism of history. I aver that history should be cleansed of the fables and absurdities which also are found in the majority of ancient writings. I aver further that we should do away with the useless and prolix material which disfigures our modern histories and is the cause that this noblest of studies is held in contempt. The annals and historical Mercuries of our times can be recommended to those who read in order to fall asleep or to dispel their thoughts. To those who read in order to profit from their reading, however, one may recommend Sallust and Tacitus among Roman writers and Polybius first and foremost among Greek writers. In their works will be found innumerable ideas from which a statesman as well as a warrior can profit.

of Ludvig Holberg

IN DEFENSE OF WALKING

EPISTLE 189

MILORD THANKS me for my last communication and says that his wife also read the letter with pleasure but that she did not approve of what I said about abolishing carriages. To her mind this would be the same as confining people to their homes, particularly ladies who would rather stay at home than trudge through Copenhagen's filthy streets and be splashed and pushed about by the common people on the streets—but his good wife did not understand me correctly. I do not at all recommend the abolition of horses and carriages. I advise only against their constant and daily use, summer as well as winter, in good weather as well as in bad. I mean only that no one should be ashamed to go through a street on foot when the weather is good. I mean that people should employ carriages when necessary but not make of them a general fashion which incommodes a city's inhabitants. I readily admit that it would be difficult for our persons of rank, particularly ladies, to make visits on foot in the city, especially since for many years, indeed almost from childhood, they have been unaccustomed to using their feet and since the streets of this city generally are unclean. I shall not cite the examples of foreign cities where the inhabitants of all classes find no difficulty in going on foot. I would say only this: that driving must not be made a matter of respectability and an absolute necessity and that ladies should go on foot when the opportunity and weather permit it, in order to demonstrate that they have feet. No serious objection can be raised against such a suggestion, for our streets are not always filthy—and were the heavy carriage traffic diminished, they would become cleaner. Nor are they very narrow; they are generally wide enough that our ladies can get through them very comfortably even though their skirts demand considerable space and several *gradus latitudinis*—the more comfortably because the streets are far from teeming with people as is the case in other large and populous cities where persons of all classes and of both sexes often go by foot and find it agreeable both to the health and the pocketbook. I wish that some distinguished matrons or young ladies would make a beginning, for others would soon make a point of following their examples. No example could have a better effect than that of Milord's own good wife, since she is praised both for her good sense and decorous habits. Persuade her first to walk through a short street in order to accustom her feet to the cobblestones and to accustom other persons to seeing her; thereafter through a longer street; and finally from one quarter of the city to another, in order to convince all the skeptical that cobblestones are not so hard and difficult to walk upon as is represented, but that the difficulty has been solely a matter of tender and unaccustomed feet. With time she doubtless would dare to go over Christianshavn's bridge to the new part of the city without Milord's having her insured. I am certain that she will like it, so well in fact that when she sees that it has become a decorous fashion also for others, she will ask Milord's permission to promenade with her daughters beyond the city's gates. When it once has become a matter of respectability, it will soon become a custom, the introduction of which can be looked upon as something advantageous, especially for the health, for there is no city known to me where corporal motion is more necessary and where persons walk less. By observing the custom, every matron would find a change in her blood the first time she was phlebotomized and every maiden that her corset would pinch less severely than previously. I shall not restate the other good effects which I mentioned in my previous communication. The only disadvantage which could come from it, would be that wheelwrights, carriage-makers, smiths, and physicians would lose some of their income by it. Shoemakers and peruke-makers, on the other hand, would flourish. Many coachmen would turn into artisans and carriage horses into mounts, and the din which is caused by constant traffic night and day would cease. I look forward to hearing what decision Milord's wife will make regarding my suggestions.

Good and Bad Comedies

Epistle 190

Milord writes that during the two months he recently spent in Copenhagen, he regularly visited our Danish theater; he complains that the same comedies were given too frequently, and is of the opinion that academic people should be encouraged either to translate the newest French and English comedies or to write some original ones. As far as translating comedies is concerned, that has often been attempted, but the translated pieces have not enjoyed success on our stage, so that it would seem that the art died with Molière. To this one can answer that the limited success which translated contemporary comedies have had, ought to be ascribed to the spectators' bad taste rather than the drama themselves, especially since it is well known that many of the modern plays, particularly those of Destouches, are received with great applause in the French theater. Yet I venture to say without vanity that our Northern audiences, especially of the middle class, are far better judges in this matter than the Parisians. If the former do not have such fine taste as the latter, they have at least a taste neither so odd nor so depraved. As proof one may adduce the following: Our public here, that does not enquire who the author is of the piece being presented, has regularly received Molière's comedies well, but rejected the translations of modern plays. Since in all countries Molière's comedies are considered to be masterpieces and since our Northern spectators can stomach only very few of the comedies written after Molière's time, one can but adjudge their taste to be good and conclude that the esteem in which the French hold their modern pieces arises from an unnatural desire for spectacular dramas—as numerous foreigners and indeed some Frenchmen have noted, and censured. Just as no one can better appreciate the delightful odor of the rose than he whose nostrils have not been vitiated by the regular use of snuff, and just as no one can enjoy the most delectable wine who has accustomed himself to coffee and lets himself believe that an infusion of water and burned beans is far more pleasant, similarly the best judges of ingenious writing and drama are those who still have their natural good taste, and who have not been convinced by others that they should renounce it. Yet this is not the sole basis for my opinion. Setting aside all prejudices, I read most of the modern plays, but I have to force myself to finish them, and the result is only that I esteem still higher than I did before the plays of Plautus and Molière. Some of my friends who have so accustomed themselves to the Parisian taste that they have lost their own, have constrained me to read numerous modern comedies, especially those of Destouches, which they consider to be masterpieces. I find them so far from being masterpieces that they do not deserve even to bear the name of drama. I observe that they do not have the constituent parts of which a comedy consists, and I find that the leading characters seldom are well delineated. I see only some disjointed scenes which do not carry the piece forward or serve the dénouement. The dialogue is tiresome and unable to arouse emotion in a spectator. All that I can praise is the style and pretty French verse—but that does not make a comedy. Try to translate the best of Destouches' dramas into prose and Milord will find that the result will be nothing but what I have sketched and will serve only to lull the spectators to sleep. Molière's comedies, on the other hand, although they too suffer in translation, always remain agreeable comedies. This is my opinion as far as translation of modern drama is concerned.

With regard to original works, experience has shown that innumerable authors have tried in vain or with limited success to write them, and therefore I cannot advise anyone to venture out into such waters. It may be said that from the age of Plautus until Molière, a period of two thousand years, no drama of note of which anything is known came into being. As far as Terence's comedies are concerned, I do not agree with those critics who make much of them and who go so far as to prefer them to the dramas of Plautus. The spirit, the gaiety, which is the soul of comedy and which animates the stage, is lacking in Terence. To be sure, his style is agreeable and the characters are well drawn, but that is something that many others can achieve too, since these qualities demand only work and a sort of judiciousness; but to write plays like Plautus demands unusual talents which are found only in few persons. Milord will perhaps find it presumptuous that I veer from the judgments of so many learned and discriminating men in this matter—but are learned and discriminating men connoisseurs of the drama? No one should or can criticize me for preferring Molière's judgment to that of the entire University of Paris. One notes that great writers of comedy have tried first and foremost to imitate Plautus and have not conformed to the criticism of learned men. One notes that of all the ancient pieces which Molière undertook to translate and rewrite, all are by Plautus and none are by Terence. It is not too much to say that Plautus' *Amphitryon, Aulularia,* and *Menechmi* still are the greatest comedies that we have. Only he who has studied the theater and felt by experience the effect of a comedy from the stage can pass judgment on a play. Since that is the case, we need not reflect on the judgments of those who sit at home and criticize in their studies without having seen a play presented. They can judge only the style, the moral saws, and the piece's conformity to rules; but experience teaches us that a comedy which follows all the academic rules is no comedy at all. Many a drama which seems to be insignificant when read can be extremely effective on the stage. A drama's importance and validity is therefore not to be measured by the criticism of learned journalists but by the applause of the spectators, and when I say spectators I mean only those who have a natural and undepraved taste. It is because of the applause of such spectators that I have a good opinion of my own dramas, for I have seen them stand up against

Molière's comedies in our theater, whereas most of the translated pieces cannot do so. That the natural good taste which our spectators have had hitherto will continue very long, I can give no assurance. It would seem that certain persons are trying to spoil it by recommending spectacular pieces meant more for the eye than the ear. That some of our distinguished ladies do not enjoy our original and domestic dramas can be ascribed principally to the catechization and tutoring of their French governesses; from childhood they have been made to read French books and they constantly converse about Parisian styles and caprices, so that it is no wonder that they do not enjoy a drama unless they see a gallooned French marquis on the stage. People of the middle class, on the other hand, whose taste has not been depraved, find greatest pleasure in those plays which criticize the country's manners and morals. I infer that their taste is the better and the more natural.

Comedies Should Be in Prose

Epistle 211

Milord writes criticizing our Danish comedies for being written in prose, whereas most foreign plays are composed in verse. I, however, look upon the prose form as symbolic and as a demonstration of the nation's natural good taste, for nothing can be more offensive than to hear commonplace everyday speech in cadence and rhyme. Such speech seems to me like laughing and crying at the same time. To this Milord can doubtless reply that the ancient Greek and Roman plays were all in verse and that no one would undertake to deny that the Romans and Greeks, particularly the Athenians, had a fine and delicate taste in the drama. Yet I do not know whether everyone would agree unless Milord perhaps referred only to blind admirers of antiquities. The dispute about the taste of the Ancients versus the taste of our times has, as far as I know, not yet been settled. I would say but this: that although one ascribe to the Ancients natural good taste in the drama, it does not follow that the versified comedies of our times are good, for it is well-known that the Greeks as well as the Romans had several kinds of verse which they employed as the subject matter required. Among the types of verse was the iambic, about which Horace speaks as follows: *syllaba longa brevi subjecta vocatur Jambus.* Since iambic verse most nearly approached prose, it was used for satires and plays and was therefore in no way repugnant. We however have only one sort of verse which is used for all kinds of subject matter and furthermore which deviates from that which is natural, for in heroic and bombastic verse everyday conversations become ridiculous. There is no doubt that the Ancients would have taken offense at this. It is therefore not by accident but because of the acumen with which nature endowed them that they chose iambic verse for drama. Only in the choruses which were between the acts was grandiloquent verse employed. The choruses are supposed to be the origin of that which we now call opera, although they were distinct from the plays and consisted of singing between the acts in order to let the actors rest and give them time to prepare for the acts to come. One may say that the instrumental music now used between the acts has succeeded the ancient chorus. Several attempts have been made to revive the chorus, but they have not won approbation. Queen Christina of Sweden, who was in love with Roman and Greek antiquities, is among those who have made such attempts. We hear that her favorite, Bourdelot, once arranged that Marcus Meibom, who had written a learned book on antique music, was to present in public a chorus in the old style and that Naudaeus was to dance afterwards. As Meibom, who was to lead the singing, had only a poor voice and, furthermore, became the subject of derision, the concert ended as a free-for-all.

The function of the ancient chorus was to moralize in song on the virtues and vices which the play suggested, so that it may be said that the chorus was to a certain extent incorporated into the drama. From this one observes that the chorus was of quite a different nature from the current opera, which is without rhyme or reason. Just as it is offensive to hear commonplace talk executed in verse, it is even less acceptable to hear it in song, so that one may state that the great pleasure many find in it can be ascribed to nothing but depraved taste.

The Best of All Possible Worlds

Epistle 232

You want to know my opinion of the dispute which has aroused so much commotion among the philosophers of our time—namely, *de mundo optimo,* that is, whether the world as it exists is the best possible world. I am not one for making decisions in philosophical disputes, and the less so where one cannot take sides without laying oneself open to dangerous criticism. Numerous respected men, among them Leibniz and Wolff, suppose that the created world is, of all worlds which God could create, the best. Leibniz tries to support his opinion with this sort of argument: God does the best that is possible, for if one teaches differently one denies either God's good will or his wisdom in choosing the best. Therefore it follows that, if the slightest evil which is seen in the world were wanting, it would no longer be the world, which in whatever condition it is now found, must be considered to be the best, since the Creator has chosen it from among all possible worlds. This doctrine is also supported by Wolff, who employs the same phraseology.

From this summary, one observes on what they base their opinions and what consequences they suppose would follow, should one disagree with them. Others have nevertheless vehemently disputed such a doctrine and deduce from it a far more dangerous consequence. They say that if God by necessity chose a plan for creation in which evil is intermixed with good, it follows that in the creation there was established the necessity of sin, and sin for which God is made responsible. (Their opponents suppose that there is a necessity in evil things in themselves, since the created world's perfection consists in an intermixture of good and evil. Thus Wolff says that the perfection of a clock consists in the harmony of all its parts, which work together toward a common goal—namely, to tell the hours.) The other party is of the opinion that evil things by no means work together with the good toward the great goal of creation that is the greater glory of God. Quite to the contrary, they say that the opposite is true. They examine Wolff's further arguments—to wit, that God made use of evil as a means which furthers the good and which makes the world a perfect machine, and furthermore that by experience one observes that some advantage is derived from a preceding misfortune. To this theory they reply, first, that it is improper to ascribe to God that which he himself censures in man and, second, that, as experience shows, it is not always true that an advantage generally derives from a preceding misfortune. One observes that each party tries to deduce dangerous consequences from its opponent's doctrine. The one party says that since the other denies that this world is the best of all possible creations, it tries to abridge God's wisdom as well as his goodness, for if the world were not the best of all possible creations, it could not have been made by a wise and good Creator. The other party derives still more dangerous consequences from the first party's opinion. Its adherents say that if one believes that the world could not have been created differently, one would abridge both God's omnipotence and free will—which in turn would strengthen the dangerous doctrine of fatality —and that God would be made subject to a fate upon which He depended and that the evil deeds of men would be excusable, since they would be performed by necessity.

To my mind the safest course is to distinguish between the earth as it was in a state of innocence and as it has become after the fall of man, for when one grants that at the dawn of creation evil was not confused with good, but that, as the Scriptures witness, everything was most excellent, the dispute can more or less be settled and the second party can agree with the first that the created world is the best, since no better can be imagined. Since Leibniz, Wolff, and their disciples speak of the world as it is now and ascertain the necessity of evil things which according to them co-operate to make the perfection that is creation, the above-named consequences must follow. They are forced to employ the doctrine of the everlasting nature of matter and say that, since matter is a mixture of good and evil, a world could not be created without such a mixture. This is really a hard nut for them to crack. They say, to be sure, that through the above-mentioned distinction the evil consequences are not neutralized, since it follows that God created a world which he knew would be brought into the state at which it arrived after the fall of man. The other party extricates itself still better and is subject to less severe objections in distinguishing between the world's original and later condition. If one could believe in chance and accept the doctrine that deeds derived from man's free will were not included in God's predestination, this problem as well as several others could be solved, but I have elsewhere shown that such a doctrine, as attractive as it may seem, is not acceptable. Since this is the case, there still remains a problem about which I consider it safest to make no absolute decision, but to count this matter among the curiosities which men let remain uninvestigated, mysteries which are and always will remain matters impenetrable by human reason.

It would be desirable, could someone compose a system by means of which these problems could be solved; he might with better cause deserve the title *Defensor fidei* than Henry VIII. I esteem those who have undertaken such a labor, for their intent has been to destroy the arguments which the Naturalists adduce against religion; but to persist too long in such an attempt, after having observed the fruitless attempts of the greatest of men, is to engage in self-contradiction and to undertake something beyond one's powers and which, for human investigation, is like unto the philosopher's stone. This admonition is for me as well as for others.

of Ludvig Holberg

Two Private Libraries
Epistle 240

Last week I visited N. N. in order to see his library, which I found in every way to correspond to the description that I had heard of it. After examining it I could but respect highly the collector for his exactness. The library is not as large as it is impressive and well arranged. Corresponding to the branches of learning which they treat, the books are distinguished by bindings in different colors. The first and leading shelf was occupied by funeral sermons all bound in black velvet; this showed that their owner looks upon them as the nucleus of his entire library, and in so doing he does nor err, for it is by funeral sermons that one is canonized and made blessed. Next was to be seen in nice order a number of other ecclesiastical works in simpler black leather bindings. There was nothing lacking in this collection except Bibles. The owner was in no hurry to acquire them, since they are always available. Thereafter were to be found in the same elegant order legal works, all bound in red, signifying the rubrics of the jurists. From this collection of legal works I observed that those persons do the good man an injustice who think him to be only a tolerable judge poorly versed in the law, for I counted nearly three hundred works in folio alone. I doubt that even the most able judge in the kingdom possesses greater legal treasures. The historical works are in mottled bindings symbolizing the diversity of history. The largest collection consists of selected novels which he has taken unbelievable pains to gather together little by little. Almost all of the novels which have been published are to be found here, and of the best of them, such as *Hercules Herculiscus, Astraea,* the story of Dr. Faust, etc., there are several editions. Works which treat economy and agriculture, and cookbooks as well, are all bound in green to suggest fields and pastures, the fruits and products of which comprise the subject matter of such books. Such a disposition serves only to demonstrate a man's ingenuity and learning. All the other books are bound in red saffian, the pleasant odor of which can refresh a sick person; and since the books are gilded on their spines, there is something both for the nose and the eye. As a consequence, strangers flock to see the library, but do not ask to see its owner. Milord will scarcely be able to contain himself for laughter when I say that the librarian is an old man who can neither read nor write, but there is good reason for this, for the books should not be dirtied by reading. The librarian has enough to do to keep them clean and to see that they do not become dusty. Nothing can be more sensible, for it is primarily for the sake of the preservation of books that librarians are employed. This librarian is reluctant to touch any book, and as a result the books all look as if they had just come from the bindery. When I wanted to take down a book, he bade me wait a moment and ran to fetch his gloves so that he would not touch the books with his bare hands. He assured me that he had not touched a single book in the entire library for three years. Milord will perhaps also laugh at this and ask of what use books are when not used, but if Milord had seen how the library was arranged, its neatness and elegant order, he would admit that one can become learned from the sight of it alone. If N. N. is not so learned as some presume, it must nevertheless be admitted that he is a lover of learning. No more striking proof of this can be given than the care with which he keeps his library; it is by such conduct that one shows esteem for scholarship. Many things seem ridiculous which upon closer examination are discovered to be well-founded. A certain man was ridiculed for several years because he generally slept in court when a case was being pleaded, but when it became known with what noble intent this happened—to wit, not to let himself be seduced by the advocates' honeyed words, it was impossible not to admire the man and not to look upon him as a fair-minded judge who observed the maxim that justice should be blind. It were desirable if others practiced the economical caution with their libraries that N. N. does, for most persons damage and dirty their books by constant use; when the books subsequently are at auction after the owner's death, they are sold for half the price which they cost. Some appraise this library at 10,000 dollars, and although it is not large, it is worth that much, for the bindings cost more than the contents. Some condemn such extravagance, but N. N. is saving in many other things. He employs no tutor for his children, and his youngest sons are kept in such frugality that two of them have only one pair of shoebuckles between them, which they use alternately, and the youngest son has neither coat nor trousers except those which an older brother has cast off after they have become too small for him. From this we observe the man's sensible economy and note that he saves with the one hand what he spends with the other.

Milord is familiar with the library of our friend Theodorus, and knows the care which has been taken in forming it and how it is treated. I recently visited his library and found there just as much negligence and disorder as I had found elegance and evidence of care in the above-mentioned library. In Theodorus' library there are to be seen intermingled on the same shelf books in white, black, and French bindings. No sight could be more repulsive. This is not all. I have seen books of an entirely different nature next to one another—for example, Danish plays next to Dr. Spener, so that it is a miracle that such incongruity has not resulted in brawls and internal wars among the books. The books bound in white are so dirtied by constant use that no respectable man who bought them would use them before they were bleached. When I saw this, I could not keep from speaking my mind to Theodorus, but he answered in cavalier fashion, "I always have to use my books; it is therefore they were purchased"—as if libraries were established and books were purchased solely for the sake of reading them. On the contrary, experience shows that the most sensible men acquire libraries for quite different reasons, intending them to be decorations and adornment for their rooms and cabinets, just as women acquire a large quantity of porcelain not to use, but solely for the sake of adorning their cupboards and chests. That which irked me most of all was to find Luther's Bible in a French binding. A hideous sight for my eyes! It was just like seeing an archdeacon in a scarlet gown. In the same library I found a large number of Latin authors. That was all right, but the nicest and most elegant editions of these authors were missing. Theodorus felt that if he had correct and accurate texts, it was enough. What dreadful taste! Just as if he were not aware that almost all literati nowadays pay most attention to the composition of a book—that is, the type, the paper, and the plates. I am ashamed to speak more of the matter here. By comparing the two libraries Milord can judge whether my opinion is well-founded or not. It is certain that strangers judge harshly in this matter, for although many of them flock to see N. N.'s library without wanting to speak to him, many visit Theodorus' house to speak with him—but not to look at a library which enjoys no prestige.

The New English Comedies

Epistle 241

I thank you for the publication you have sent me which contains remarks about the English and the French nations. Not without good reason does the author give preference in most things to the English. Their plays, however, do not please him, and I subscribe readily to the judgment which he passes on them. I have on the occasion of the re-establishment of the Danish theater leafed through several English comedies in order to see whether any of them could serve our purpose, but as yet I have found none which could be successfully presented at our theater—and for a variety of reasons. First of all, there is found in most English plays so much courtship that one becomes confused in reading a play and cannot concentrate one's thoughts. In the second place, they are all full of difficult and pompous expressions which one does not comprehend at first glance. Finally, other nations find their comparisons repulsive. For example, instead of saying, "She hated him like death," the English express themselves thus: "She hates him worse than a Quaker hates a Parrot or than a Fishmonger hates a hard Frost." Instead of saying, "They squabbled and sputtered at one another," the English say: "Sputt'ring at one another like two roasting apples." The English plays are full of such metaphors. I would not dispute the nation its taste on this account, but I remark only that other nations find such grandiloquence loathsome. I will not even mention the obscenities which are found in the English plays, for many of them would be intolerable to gentlemen, to say nothing of our fair ladies who must loosen their corsets when they but hear the word "virginity" or anything similar spoken from the stage.

The Sciences in China

Epistle 254

I AM HAPPY that Milord is pleased with what I wrote about China. He says in his last communication, however, that he cannot reconcile other laudatory reports about the sciences in China with what I have written about the respect which the Jesuits have won for themselves in that country by instructing the Chinese in many important matters of which they previously had no knowledge. The reports must be understood to refer only to instruction in mathematics, music, and certain other branches of learning in which the Chinese have made no particular progress. Missionaries witness that the Chinese regularly have excelled in astronomy, the history of their own country, and ethics. With regard to astronomy, it must be admitted that no people has applied itself more assiduously to that science, for the astronomical observations of the Chinese are as old as their empire. Their history shows that they always have maintained men whose task it is to observe everything that happens in the heavens day and night.

It is such a serious matter to them that observers who show the slightest negligence in the performance of such duties are punished with their lives. The Jesuits, who were at first incredulous, have examined the oldest astronomical calculations of the Chinese, and to their astonishment found them quite correct. There are exact descriptions of constellations, eclipses, equinoxes, and solstices which were observed 120 B.C., and in one work there is noted the first observation of an eclipse of the sun, in the year 2155 B.C. They have also observed various new stars and comets which Europeans have not seen. P. Ricci witnesses that in the ancient observatory at Nanking there were instruments the like of which were not to be found in Europe. According to the description of the Peking observatory made by P. Lecomte, nothing can be more splendid. In that city are maintained throughout the year five mathematicians who observe the heavens day and night and record what they see with such accuracy that one can only be astonished at it. From this we observe that the ignorance of sciences which is ascribed to the Chinese does not extend to astronomy, to which they have applied themselves more than any European nation. The same can be said of history. No other people has been so vigilant in preserving its historical writings. They have an uninterrupted history of several thousand years, from the establishment of the empire until the present day. A number of scholars have regularly been commissioned to observe and write down all the emperor's words and acts. Each historian compiles his work independently, without showing it to the others, and deposits what he has written through an aperture in a chest. As such writings are not published until a long time has passed and not until the reigning imperial house no longer is on the throne, everything is found to be recorded with candor. As soon as the crown passes from one imperial family to another, all the preserved reports are collected and compared with one another in order to deduce the truth upon which an emperor's history may be based. In addition, every city records in print everything remarkable which comes to pass in the district where it is located. Such works give a description of the place, and tell of the inhabitants, of their customs and pursuits, and of persons who have distinguished themselves by learning or in military affairs. By such precaution, reliable histories can and must be secured. It is different with us. Here everyone who can write undertakes to write histories, and as a consequence there are but few that are satisfactory and reliable among the many which we have. Besides truthful histories, the Chinese also have a number of novels which do not comprise mere love stories alone in the fashion of our novels, but contain moral teachings. Their novels are therefore as useful for youth as ours are detrimental. P. Dentrecolle has translated three or four such novels which are included in Du Halde's great work. One of these novels has the same content as the well-known story we have about the Ephesian matron who feigned she would not live after the death of her husband and therefore sat day and night at his grave without food or drink but shortly thereafter entered into a disreputable marriage with an officer. In the Chinese novel the husband is said to have lain several days in a torpor and then to have awakened unexpectedly just as his presumed widow was preparing to share the bed of the new bridegroom. The best of these novels generally conclude with some verses. The didactic works of the Chinese are excellent. First and foremost they stress a subject's respect for the government and obedience by children and servants towards parents and masters. They choose examples from history and praise the heroic deeds of various virtuous men as worthy of emulation.

The government in China is so artfully constituted that one cannot observe its orderliness and elegance without astonishment. From all this one sees in how far they are right who have spoken laudably of the Chinese people but at the same time what the basis is for the charge of ignorance made by the present missionaries, for in logic, rhetoric, and music they have made only tolerable progress. In particular they have neglected practical geometry, and it is especially on that account that the Jesuits have acquired such great prestige in China.

Changes in the English Character

Epistle 260

I RECENTLY SPOKE with a young gentleman who had spent some time in Spain. He told me that the Spanish nation has recently become almost unrecognizable. He declared that the former Spanish gravity has been transmuted into French capriciousness and that life in Madrid is almost the same as in Paris. This corroborates what I previously have noted about human inclination, namely that location, air, and food are of little or no consequence, but that it is government, laws, and ordinances alone that fashion men and cast them into another form, for in a short time an entire people can be seen to become unlike its former self; decorum is changed into capriciousness, melancholy into lack of restraint, cowardice into courage, and vice versa.

No nation is a more striking example of this than the English. Englishmen, who in olden times seemed to be created for slavery, are now the boldest of all European peoples and the greatest lovers of freedom. When one considers England's former condition, particularly at the time of William the Conqueror, one is astonished at the people's patience and blind obedience toward the government. One cannot read the history of those times without dolefulness, for one finds that the English let themselves be subjugated by a small and insignificant foreign people, the Normans, and acquiesced with such patience in all the violence, scorn, and contempt to which they were subjected that scarcely any Oriental nation could produce a more striking example. Now, on the other hand, their boldness knows no limits, and most Englishmen's desire for freedom is so great that the citizens of no other country show anything similar. In various places in my works I have spoken of the freedom which certain persons assume in speaking and writing against the government, and in publishing bitter criticism of ordinances and establishments made by the King and Parliament in war and peace. This is not even permitted in Holland or any other free republic. Most Englishmen will not let themselves be coerced in any matter, and experience teaches that coercion serves only to increase their audacity. In one of my Latin epistles I have drawn a portrait of that nation, so I shall not go further into the matter here. I will only note here that in London there always are to be found writers who in weekly or monthly journals disparage the undertakings of the court and the decisions of Parliament. They who are plying this trade with the greatest freedom are above all two authors, one who bears the name of *Craftsman* and the other whose periodical is entitled *Old England.* Both these writers publish everything that occurs to them, and quite without hesitation, even regarding the most delicate affairs of state. As an example I shall cite only one such audacious criticism which I recently read in an issue of the publication entitled *Old England.* It is well-known that for several years England has been trying to get Holland openly to declare herself against France. The government considered this a most necessary thing for England and all the allies. At the same time that this effort is being made, the author of *Old England* makes fun of it, saying that they are trying to hoodwink Holland and that it is not to Holland's welfare and best interest to lend an ear to such demands. However great a patron of freedom one is, one must admit that this goes too far and is in conflict with the well-being of organized society. The worst of it is that these authors often are befogged in their reasoning and baseless in their statements, just as *Old England* in this case, for he says that it would serve Holland's interest to seek perpetual friendship with France and that France has neither the will nor the ability to subjugate the republic—but that is contrary to all evidence. Time has shown that Holland would have done better to listen to the English representations in good season. Such writing is to be condoned no more than the

Duchess of Marlborough's will, which gave £100,000 to William Pitt because he continually had censured the acts of the Court and of Parliament.

Bayle and the Epicurean Societies

Epistle 335

In my *Journey to the World Underground* I have depicted a republic consisting of atheists and, in describing it, shown how necessary religion is for the vigor and preservation of society. One of M. Bayle's paradoxes which he elaborates with scintillating arguments is that a society very well can exist without religion. He cites as proof the Epicurean societies in which was found as great an abundance of friendly intercourse and harmony as a lack of religion, so that unbelief and virtue ruled to an equal degree. His description is as follows: Epicurus established a school in a pretty garden which he had purchased. There he lived with his friends in peace and amicable companionship. Since it was believed that no society was better organized, people flocked from Greece, Egypt, and Asia in order to become members of it. Quarreling, greed, envy, hate, and all the vices were banished from there. All were of one mind and one will, and lived with one another in such friendly intercourse that we read about the society with astonishment. Cicero says that from the time of Theseus until Orestes one could find only two or three examples of such sincere friendship as that which reigned among the disciples of Epicurus, who did not believe in any Divine Providence. On the other hand, among members of other philosophic sects, even the Stoic, one saw hate, envy, and dissension.

Now, says Bayle, let someone come forth and proclaim that societies cannot exist without religion. To be sure, the Epicureans did not deny the existence of gods, but since they looked upon them only as beautiful beings who did not meddle with the regimen of the world and as beings which, like other creatures, were mortal, religion for the Epicureans existed in name only, and the devotion and piety which they displayed were based only on a kind of propriety which had to be observed in order not to offend the public. The patrons of unbelief employ this argument in order to give us a still better impression about these societies. When Diocles saw with what reverence Epicurus worshipped the gods, he cried aloud, "What a sight for me to see this man in a temple! Now all my suspicions toward him disappear; I have never admired God's majesty and magnificence more than now that I see Epicurus lying at His feet." What he meant was this: Look, here is a man who is worshipping God in a disinterested way without regard to punishment or reward, a man who honors Him alone because He is deserving of the honor, whereas others practice such worship either because of fear or punishment, or in hope of reward, and that cannot be called unselfish worship of God.

The patrons of unbelief assemble this sort of evidence in order to show that they who deny Divine Providence not only can be good citizens but even pious members of society. I do not venture to deny that which is adduced about the Epicurean societies or to call their history a fiction, but I do not believe that the claims of infidels receive any support whatsoever from it. It is one thing when certain chosen persons join in an association and then live constantly under the supervision and daily cathechization of a master, for through this they are encouraged to observe the founder's rules. It is quite another thing to find harmony outside such closed bodies and within great nations. Even robbers and freebooters religiously observe the laws of their organizations, but from this fact can be deduced only that they can and should be looked upon as the sworn enemies of all mankind. Other proof is needed in order to strengthen the above-mentioned claim. The test must be made outside such bodies and in ordinary societies and places. I am of the opinion that this never has been done. On the contrary, history provides us with many examples, and common sense teaches us, that few persons eschew sins which they consider to be unpunishable or to lie beyond the jurisdiction of secular authority. Furthermore experience shows that to practice virtue solely for the love of virtue and to eschew vices solely because they are vices is but a *façon de parler.* Such prattle is as ill-founded as that of the Stoics who say that man can disassociate himself from all emotions—that is to say, cease being man.

On Translating Epistle 342

In the preface to my translation of Herodian, I mentioned several important rules which must be observed by persons who would translate books. Among such rules is the following: with regard to style one must not follow the original too closely, for every language has its character, and elegance in one language may be the disfigurement of another. For this reason one must beware of all too literal translations which make a language seem ridiculous and distorted. Some critics have complained that Northern authors do not endeavor to write elegantly and gracefully. These in turn rebuke others for their pondered and ornamental style, a style which often indicates that more attention is being paid to form than to subject matter. It is therefore that the simplicity of Comineus, Montaigne, *et al.,* is preferable to the scintillating histories and moral writings of many other authors. We observe that the ancient Romans, who were men of reason, had such a plain taste and that they therefore looked upon the so-called elegant writers as corrupters of the language. I take no side in the matter, for I prefer to go a middle path. I would say only that I do not read certain florid French and Italian books with the same pleasure as other persons who are so beguiled by the style that they pay little attention to the subject matter. I have observed that many works which strike the public's fancy are of little importance when the gilt wears off, gilt which consists of metaphors, so-called witticisms *(pointes)*, and favorite *façons de parler*, and which makes a book glitter as feathers the peacock. The peacock's feathers have to make up for his lack of song and for the rest of his body, which in itself has nothing particular to recommend it. The Italians find in Oriental writings splendid and intricate expressions which they cannot imitate without deforming their own language. The French find Italian books too full of affectation; and the Northern peoples, whose style is simple and natural, in turn reject French elegancies which in their languages lose their virtue and no longer are elegant. I have seen some literal Danish translations of certain French works; nothing seems more ridiculous to me than for "lengthy ratiocination," for example, to say "a flood or deluge of *raisons*." The latter is an elegant French expression, but it is unpalatable in our language. Similarly, it is ridiculous to say for "I adopt this opinion," "I am wedded to this opinion," and to employ innumerable phrases of this sort.

I do not condemn these embellishments and ornate expressions; I say only that they are not acceptable in our language until Danish ears become accustomed to them. If it be maintained that our authors gradually must accustom themselves to such expressions, I would reply that I am not sure there is any necessity of it. No one can reject a work in which the subject matter is well presented in a natural and simple style. The most ornate works are not the most substantial. It would seem that petty writers employ external ornamentation and embellishment in order to give their subject matter a prestige which it does not actually have, just as incompetent and contemptible persons necessarily clothe themselves in gallooned garments in order to be taken for what they are not. The French speak of the simplicity of their language, but foreigners are unable to perceive it; similarly, in their verse the French pride themselves on observing rules of prosody for which others can find no evidence. However simple and natural the French suppose their language to be, it is certain that the Germans, the Danes, and the Swedes cannot make use of literal translations from the French. What irks me is that in their clever works *(ouvrages d'esprit)* there are far too many favorite *façons de parler;* the one writer seems to have copied from the other and the symmetry of style seems everywhere to be the same. It is as with their music; when one has heard one French overture, one has heard almost all of them.

The Attributes of a Teacher

Epistle 390

Milord wants me to suggest someone to tutor his children. This is a commission which I am reluctant to accept, for the position of tutor is of greater importance than generally is believed. Most tutors are judged by their erudition, as if that were enough, providing they otherwise have no faults or vices. Erudition is necessary, to be sure, but I do not reckon it among the principal qualities which are to be required of a pedagogue. I would seek in the first instance a person gifted with acumen and moderation. Although only moderately learned, someone possessing these two attributes can effect far more than the most learned individual to be found at a university. Learning and wisdom are two different qualities; we know by experience that a man can be just as unreasonable as he is learned. It follows that an erudite tutor who does not possess enough acumen to gain insight into the disposition of his pupil is wasting time by teaching the pupil things he later will have to forget. Here, as in architecture, it is of primary importance to examine the ground before raising and building. When the tutor is chosen because of his powers of discernment and when every child's peculiarities, aptitudes, and natural talents are ascertained before the child is set out on a path leading to some goal, then happy and rapid progress can be expected. Most tutors fail to consider such things. Almost every one of them takes his own schooling as a model, without reflecting that the work to be done depends on the nature of the material, and that different instruments are used to cut wood than to cut steel. Artisans, artists, agriculturalists, and the like all keep this in mind. A builder examines the ground before constructing a building and sees to it that every stone is put in a place where it can be to best advantage. An artist examines his raw material before working with it; and a farmer does not simply follow his predecessor's example; he examines the soil to see for what crop it is best suited. When I find that soil is not suitable for wheat or rye, I sow barley or oats. In short, all take existing conditions into consideration. Only they who are entrusted with the instruction of the young and whose function it is to cultivate human beings confound their ideal with their charges' needs. Consequently there is superimposed upon young persons a form which does not correspond to their nature, so that they must be reduced to raw material again and recast in another form. Certain rulers and legislators have sought to prevent this and have therefore named officials in every city who should oversee the training of youth and see to it that every child was properly placed and instructed in that subject for which nature has predestined him. This admirable practice is said to have prevailed in ancient Egypt, Persia, and Greece; and the Chinese are said still to observe it. It would insure that the years of youth are not wasted and that rapid and happy progress in studies is effected, for a child requires reins rather than spurs in the subject which is to his liking and for which he has a natural inclination.

The other principal quality demanded of a school teacher is moderation, for it is through gentleness and friendly intercourse that the hearts of the pupils are won. If the pupil is fond of his teachers, the desire to study results. Similarly, severity and tyranny breed an antipathy toward study. The testimonial which the citizens of the subterranean city of Keba gave a student who sought the position of schoolmaster is therefore not ill-founded, although with regard to style and form it evokes a reader's laughter. What it means is that if a teacher is not pleasant to associate with and is not gifted with patience and moderation, he is, for all his learning, not fitted to occupy his office. Friendly exhortation is more effective than the ferule and the birch rod. Those school teachers are especially to be reprimanded who cane children indiscriminately, that is, punish some because they are unable to comprehend and learn as rapidly as others. Such teachers forget that nature does not distribute the same gifts equally to everyone. Such conduct, which unfortunately is that of most teachers, is just as foolish as that of a sculptor who curses, scolds, and becomes angry because it is more difficult to give form to metal and stone than to wood or wax.

The Freedom of the Press

Epistle 395

A Swedish gentleman passing through our city honored me with a visit and related that in Sweden it had been debated whether it was advisable to give authors the freedom they enjoy in England and the Netherlands, or whether writings should continue to be subjected to censorship. He said that he, together with many others, had advocated the former principle but that there was a plurality for the latter. In this as in most matters, there can be cited arguments both pro and con. On the one hand it can be asserted that much bad and scandalous writing is suppressed by censorship, but on the other hand it can be said that many splendid books which are a nation's pride would have remained unknown forever, had censors been the order of the day everywhere. I have often recommended freedom of the press and looked upon censorship as the chains and fetters of the learned world. I have, on the other hand, been of the opinion that freedom of the press should be granted only to those who have achieved maturity, and I have become even more convinced of this after having observed young persons writing about the most delicate matters, political as well as moral, before they have grown a beard. To them one should say with David: Let them stay in Jericho until their beards grow. It may be objected that certain young persons are mature early, so that they have acquired sufficient discrimination at an early age—but this is rare indeed and although such ability can be found in youth, it is nevertheless offensive when young persons assume the role of teachers in important matters, and when they would reform the world before they have got to know it. I therefore approve the subterranean ordinance requiring a certain age for such undertaking. Otherwise I do not have much use for the customary censors, for I note that trivial works are published and numerous admirable ones remain hidden. It is certain that had censorship existed where Erasmus, Grotius, Montaigne, Le Clerc, Bayle, and certain other great men lived and wrote, their manuscripts which, like their heterodoxy, contained so much that is useful, would have remained hidden and have mouldered away so that the wheat would have been destroyed with the tares.

Queen Anne and Queen Elizabeth

Epistle 400

Milord writes that he recently has read my *Histories of Great Women* and expresses wonder that, while I have written about several English queens, I have forgotten Queen Anne, whose reign he thinks in every way to have been quite as illustrious as Elizabeth's. He enumerates as proof (1) her splendid victories, whereby the great French King Louis XIV (who previously had been the dismay of all Europe) was forced to accept the stipulations which Queen Anne granted him and to give *carte blanche* in order to save his kingdom; (2) the many and almost invincible fortresses conquered in the Netherlands, which eventually opened the way to Paris for her; (3) her authority in pacifying all of quarreling Europe and forcing everyone to make peace according to a plan of her design; (4) the union of England and Scotland, an accomplishment toward which all of her predecessors had striven in vain.

It cannot be denied that great things were brought about

during her reign and that she deserves to have a place among the most renowned women of history, but in my book I did not undertake to write about all, but only some certain distinguished women who could be tolerably well paired together because of the similarities of their deeds as well as their personal qualities. I consider Queen Anne to have been one of the most illustrious queens of England, but I can by no means agree with Milord that she takes precedence over Queen Elizabeth. One has but to compare their respective deeds and personal qualities to see that the scales are unequally weighted. With regard to the achievements of Queen Anne which have been cited, they are indeed great, but let us briefly compare them with Elizabeth's. Both had to confront the mightiest monarchs of their times. King Philip II was just as great a dismay to Europe as later King Louis XIV, so that it was equally difficult to check the former and the latter. Both queens humiliated a great warlord; the difference was that Elizabeth did it with her own forces, whereas Anne was supported by the Emperor, by Holland, Portugal, Savoy, and many of the German princes. The condition of Europe was such that Anne was supported by as many friends and accomplices as Elizabeth was surrounded by enemies, so we note that Elizabeth triumphed because of her own might and peculiar skill in governing. The great victory which was won over Philip's invincible armada may be laid against the battles of Höchstädt and Ramillies. I allow that both queens' military achievements were equally great; but consider how many other great things were achieved by Elizabeth which made her reign so illustrious. It was through her courage and alertness that the foundation was laid for the republic of the United Provinces of the Netherlands, which still flourish. It was because of her diligence that new colonies were established in America, that trade prospered, and that the foundation thus was laid for England's strength and wealth. It was because of her solicitousness that Protestantism was established and took root in England and that arts and industries were begun. In short, it was Elizabeth's illustrious reign which endowed England with the wealth by means of which Elizabeth's successors have been able to keep a balance of power in Europe. If one now considers both queens' personal qualities, one finds that Elizabeth's everywhere were more brilliant and of greater significance, so that if Anne was an illustrious queen, then Elizabeth was a ruler whose equal is scarcely to be found in history.

Oysters on Trees

Epistle 433

I was recently in a company of persons where a traveler related that there were certain countries where oysters are to be seen growing on trees. Those present smiled at this and one of them replied that there were also certain lakes where one can fish for cabbages, apples, and pears. The second statement, as ridiculous as it was, seemed more acceptable than the first to those who were present. So it goes, as one might demonstrate by numerous examples. A seafaring man once was asked by some peasants why the moon sometimes underwent an eclipse. He explained to them that this occurred when the earth passed between the sun and the moon and cast its shadow on the moon. Thereupon his hearers all burst into laughter and would speak no more of the matter. Finally another peasant asked why it was that the moon waxes and wanes. The seaman, who observed that it was easier to hoax them than to convince them of the truth, then said that the cause of the change was that, as the moon grew, pieces were cut off in order to make stars. This the peasants believed and thanked him for the intelligence. As far as oysters are concerned, the traveler's statement about them is quite true, for in the Antilles there are to be found trees which are so full of oysters that branches are broken off by their weight. These oysters do not differ from other oysters in flavor. Childrey, an Englishman, reports that this also is the case at Plymouth. Oyster seed that grows and lives on trees is occasionally thrown up on land by the sea. In China there is a small sort of oyster which the Chinese sow in certain fields where the oysters grow under water. I shall omit listing further proof and say only that it must have been a bold man who first dared swallow raw oysters. Eating oysters is even stranger than eating raw meat—a practice for which certain nations are reproached.

Three Kinds of Comedies

Epistle 441

The several contradictory opinions and judgments which daily are passed on our plays oblige me so frequently to touch on the subject, although against my will. The disputers can be divided into three sects. The first wants moral comedies with an admixture of hilarity—that is, of a sort which at the same time instructs and amuses. Furthermore, this sect wants comedies in which the dramatic rules prescribed by Aristotle and other masters are observed, so that every piece contains a coherent plot. This same sect considers it necessary that the argument be simple, without the complications of love and courtship which confuse spectators when English plays and various French pieces are presented; furthermore, that there must be protasis, epitasis, and catastrophe, without which a comedy cannot be given the name of comedy; and finally that above all there must prevail the spirit of gaiety which is the very soul of comedy and which pervades the plays of Plautus, Molière, and some few others. There are but few such pieces, since they demand a natural talent which cannot be acquired by study. Some of these comedies delineate certain leading characters, others are concerned only with humorous plots, but some are at the same time didactic. Since this kind of play is for the ear as well as the eye, discriminating spectators have hitherto found it most to their taste. The sect wanting this sort of play can be called orthodox, since it demands order and rules, *utile* and *dulce*—that is, utility intermingled with pleasure.

The second sect consists of those spectators who want comedies which appeal to the eye alone. It is no great art to satisfy them: a master of theatrical machinery is better at such a task than the best writer of comedy. Of a nature which suits the taste of the sect are several comedies which it has been found necessary to present on our stage often in order to lure spectators. Among them are *The Bewitched Bowl, Vulcan's Rod, The Oracle,* and other similar incoherent pieces which cannot be played without costly costumes and machinery; discriminating people do not find these pieces to their taste to read. Despite its weaknesses, this sort of comedy is not entirely to be rejected, since it does have a certain function in delighting the eye and arousing laughter. Since I have noted that most time and energy is expended on such performances, I have often (although in vain) pleaded for moderation, so that a useful establishment should not degenerate into pure harlequinade.

The third sect consists of the kind of spectators who find only the *à la mode* Parisian plays to their taste, plays generally of such a nature that it is scarcely possible to retell their contents after they have been seen or read, for they lack a coherent plot and the three divisions required in the traditional comedy. They consist only of some ornate conversations and are of such a quality that anyone who writes a nice style is able to forge such pieces. Experience shows that in order to write comedies special genius and innate qualities are necessary. It would seem that this last kind of play is of such a nature that (as the author of the weekly French paper which has been published here under the title of *Aspasie* thinks) the Danes are unable to produce them, either because of the nation's ineptitude and lack of proper taste or because of the simplicity of the language. If the author of *Aspasie* believes this is a matter of taste, he does the nation no little honor, contrary to his intent, for the new *à la mode* French plays do not win the approbation of the discriminating spectator or reader. I for my part can testify that I have been able to read none of such pieces without disgust. Our critic will presumably reply that, had I the fine and delicate taste that he has, I would judge differently. I would counter that, in the first place, I am not certain how far he is capable of judging in such matters and, in the second, that the more sensible critics, not only foreigners but also Frenchmen, agree with me in this matter. In Paris I have heard French as well as Italian actors speak with contempt of the fashionable plays which they have to stage to satisfy the depraved and unnatural taste of certain *petits-maîtres.* That the apologists of the fashionable drama do not dare openly to speak with contempt of Molière's comedies may be ascribed only to his reputation, for if a new work were to be written in Molière's style, they would frown on it. It is here as in music: Corelli's compositions are respected everywhere because they are by Corelli; but other pieces, although in the same style and of the same nature, are found cacophonous. The reason that certain persons express contempt for older plays and admire newer ones may in part be merely human inconstancy—*toujours chapon* as it were—and in part the fact that they see their own weaknesses portrayed in the good old plays. It is therefore that plays like *Jean de France* are for them as disagreeable as thunder for a troll and light for an owl. When one asks them how they can admire the new plays which every author can devise and in which there is found nothing that instructs or amuses, no order, and nothing either for eye or ear save the ornate style, they reply that it is in such pieces that an actor can properly demonstrate his adroitness and art, whereas in the older plays even a poor comedian can win applause. That is the same as saying that soup made from a meat skewer is better than chicken soup because it requires greater art to make the former tasty than the latter.

I speak with ardor, for I consider it my duty to declaim against depraved taste, which, like a contagious disease, can infect entire nations if timely admonitions are not made. If anyone objects, saying that I am acting against my own principle, which is not to dispute another's taste, I reply that my principle is upheld rather, since I speak against those who would force their taste upon others and move others to admire things which are based upon passing fashions and for which no natural reasons are given or can be given. Milord enquires whether our original plays are now presented with the same success as previously. This could not be expected, since they have been in print and in everyone's hands for many years and since the translated French pieces, although older, now pass for new. None the less, the former have paid higher profits than the latter. Yet it must be said that our original plays have never been in greater danger of losing their high repute than nowadays, for all efforts are exerted to enhance the reputation of the translated French plays, the staging of which is so expensive that it is to be feared the theater will be strangled at birth by the debts incurred. Although it is none of my business, I have from time to time uttered admonitions, for I have learned by experience that the receipts of plays are greater the first three years they are given than in the ten following years and that one must forthwith assemble a capital which can act as a counterbalance to lean years to come. Results will show that these my suggestions, so often made in vain, have not been ill-founded.

The Art of Flying

Epistle 452

Men have long tried in vain to acquire the arts of making gold and of flying. From the tale which Milord recently related to me, one concludes that certain persons still fancy that the latter is possible and that by taking on artificial wings it is possible to sweep up into the air after the fashion of birds. If these foolish people would consider the difference between a man's heavy body and a bird's light body and if they would carefully examine the formation of a bird's wings, the tail which the bird employs as a rudder, and various other attributes with which nature alone has endowed and can endow birds, they would not undertake an experiment which cannot succeed and, what is more, can be more harmful than useful and have the same effect as alchemy—about which I have previously written. It is credible that God has put these things out of reach for the human race for, if men could learn to fly, the whole world would take on a different appearance. Men would have to flee their cities and villages and dig themselves holes in the grounds after the fashion of birds of prey, for walls and fortifications would not protect one man against another's violence. In short, governments, societies, and pacts would cease, for they would be of no avail, and men would be seen only in holes in the ground or on peaks of mountains whence they would fly down in order to plunder and to return with their booty, so that the attribute which man begrudges animals would, if acquired, only bring about his own destruction.

L'Homme Machine

Epistle 467

Milord is astonished at the mild judgment which I pass on the author of the book entitled *L'Homme Machine.* I pass no mild judgment on an author who rejects both religion and ethics. I say only that, since he apparently has arrived at his strange opinions through all too subtle speculations, and seems to have drowned in his own wisdom, as it were, he is less to be censured than certain other writers who have mocked religion out of wantonness and who believe nothing because they will believe nothing. The former can be linked to a drunken man whose brain is befogged by too strong drink, or to someone whose vision has been impaired by too much reading; the latter, on the other hand, can be likened to those who have eyes but will not see and have reason but will not use it. *L'Homme Machine* is indeed one of the most abominable publications which have come to light for some time. It contains numerous arguments which, although ill-founded, have a semblance of truth. One must admit that learning which is based on experience is the most dependable criterion. One must also agree that organs of the body, the blood, and the humors contribute to that which is called reason and that they affect the emotions and inclinations. Since this is the case, we see what has led the author astray and engendered the dangerous convictions which make him deny the soul and its effects, and declare it to be a mere chimera and nonentity, convictions which make him ascribe to the body all that which otherwise is ascribed to the soul. Even though one admit the effects of the blood and the humors in a human being, it does not follow that the soul does not exist or that the organic constitution of the body is the source of man's merits. Despite all the experiments which he cites and by means of which he tries to show that each person's will and inclinations correspond to his physical constitution, there nevertheless remains something in the person which cannot be attributed to bodily mechanism—to wit, the struggle between the flesh and the spirit, as the Scriptures put it. Every person can say of himself, *Video meliora proboque, deteriora sequor,* i.e., "I see and subscribe to the good but practice evil." We observe that even in a paroxysm caused by the fermentation of the blood and by mental confusion, the human being often can temper an emotion or at least judge that it should be tempered. The ability to think can be restricted by physical disability, but it cannot be stifled entirely, as we know by experience—which is the author's criterion. Experience can thus be cited as proof for both sides of the argument. Such ability to think is rather anti-machinistic and demonstrates that man consists of something other than pure matter. Just as experience shows what effect the structure of the human body can have, it likewise shows that a human being is something recalcitrant and that man has a duality or double source. If this were not the case, there would be no struggle and everything would drift along like a ship before the wind when there is no pilot at the rudder.

The constitution of the body must therefore be compared to the wind which drives the ship onto skerries and rocks, whereas the soul is to be compared to the pilot who tries to prevent shipwreck. From this we see the author's extravagances. All that we can grant him is that in the adjudging of misdeeds, punishment can be tempered according to the malefactor's constitution and that, although two persons are guilty of the same misdeed, they should not suffer the same punishment, since one has violent emotions to combat, where the other sins of free will.

Parisian Politeness

Epistle 483

No city has a greater reputation for *politesse* than Paris, and it is primarily for that reason that our youth is sent thither; but it seems to me that *politesse* and elegant habits are confounded with audacity and that which we call impertinence. I for my part can say that I nowhere have heard more shameless speech than in Paris. Among members of the middle class I have experienced a sullenness at which I have often taken offense. The expressions *allez* and *vous vous moquez de moi* and others which one constantly hears can but grate on the ears of other nations. When I have asked about a rare book in bookstores, for example, I have often received the reply, *On le garde pour vous.* As far as cleanliness is concerned, no city in Europe which is known to me has less to boast of. Among the middle class it is not unusual for people to sleep a whole week in beds that have not been made; and their privies are such that I blush to speak of them. To be sure, one sees persons of only moderately high rank in gallooned clothing and lackeys with gold-clocked stockings—but at the same time with shirts so dirty a Dutch seaman would not wear them. The modesty which so adorns our Northern ladies is there called *impolitesse* and that which is there called elegance consists in sitting with crossed legs, singing songs in company, and cursing, for no city has a greater store of oaths. Since man and wife are almost never seen together paying visits, the Parisian marriage ceremony should be formulated in this way: What marriage puts asunder let no man join! This last condition prevails with everyone, particularly persons of high rank. In conclusion, I shall cite the portrait which a witty author has given of a distinguished gentleman, for it can fit a person of high rank in Paris: He never plays cards, except on Sunday, and when someone demands money of him he excuses himself with his baronial title. When we take this into consideration we see that what the Parisians call *politesse* is nothing but brazenness through which order and propriety are violated. I do not deny the Parisians' good qualities, but I do not believe that it is necessary to enumerate them, since the Parisians themselves never fail to speak of them.

Moliere's Comedies and Mine

Epistle 506a

On several occasions I have expressed my thoughts about the modern comedies which have made their appearance since the time of Molière. I have also pointed out the reason why there is such a discrepancy between the plays of this and the previous century—to wit, the bad taste of the spectators of our times. Writers of comedy must conform to the taste of the spectators, so that the fault lies not with the former but with the latter, although it must be admitted that the talent to write drama is found only in few persons. Nevertheless, many attempt it nowadays without reflecting that to write a drama requires an unusual and innate ability and that an entire century scarcely can produce one such spirit as Molière's. Another reason for the poverty of the contemporary comedy may also be adduced: when Molière undertook to write dramas there was a large and rich store of Spanish and Italian comedies which, although they were without form, served as a stimulus for the writing of good comedies, so that Molière had but to recast them. This he did with such facility that, although they are not original, his plays can pass for original comedies. From the list which Riccoboni has made of the old Spanish and Italian comedies, it may be seen that most of the characters which writers of comedy may employ appear in them, and that Molière took the subject matter of almost all of his plays from the older comedies. Thus his *L'Étourdi* or *Fantast* is an imitation of the Italian piece called *L'inavertito* written by Nicolo Barbieri; his *Dépit amoureux* or *The Amorous Quarrel* is after another Italian play, *L'Amoroso sdegno. Le Medicin malgré lui* is after an old Italian piece *Arlichino Medico non Volento; Pourceaugnac* after *Disgrazie d'Arlichino; Tartuffe* after *il Dottor Bachettone; L'École des maris* and *George Dandin* are after two older pieces; *Sganarelle* is after *Arlichino Cornuto per opinione; Festin de Pierre, or, The Ungodly Man* after a Spanish drama; the two principal comedies, *The Miser* and *Amphitryon,* are after Plautus—and so forth. There are but few of Molière's comedies where he did not find a way prepared for him, but it must be admitted that he altered his models in such a way that his comedies can pass for original works. From this it may nevertheless be concluded that it is the more difficult for modern writers of comedy to produce good plays, since the best characters have been overworked. They who, although lacking Molière's spirit, have attempted to take Molière's characters and the characters of some few of his successors as models for the modern drama, have succeeded only in spoiling such characters. No one can judge better in this matter than I who have written over thirty dramas. It has been most difficult for me to invent characters not previously delineated by others. My work has, however, not been in vain, as may be shown by the following of my comedies which have been published: *The Political Tinker, or, Statesman in His Own Imagination; The Weathercock* (for it is far older than Destouches' *Irresolu); Gert Westphaler; The Delivery Room* (in which are shown the inconveniences caused by visiting women in childbed); *The Arabian Powder; Ulysses,* which satirizes the amorphous market comedies; *Melampe,* which is a satire on tragedies, and in which a petty and ridiculous subject is treated in grandiloquent verse; also the comedy entitled *Neither Head nor Tail,* which shows how a change of character can make persons go to extremes; *False Alarm,* which shows how a petty thing can stir up an entire nation and how a petty lie can grow; *The Fussy Man; Honnête Ambition,* about the climber who knows how to excuse his aspirations; and *Don Ranudo, or, Genteel Poverty.* These are my printed comedies of character. As yet unprinted are *Plutus* (the argument for which is, to be sure, taken from the ancient Greek poet Aristophanes, although my comedy bears no resemblance to his, since it elaborates an unusual and paradoxical moral and must therefore pass for an original work); *Philosopher in his own Imagination;* and *The Republic, or, the Common Good,* which satirizes project-makers. My other plays, which are but amusing tales, are nevertheless full of critical and moral teachings, so that I think the entire production is not unworthy of a philosopher and an old man.

Montesquieu and His Theory of Climate

Epistle 516

In various places in my works and particularly in my *Histories of Heroes,* I have shown that the difference between nations with regard to virtue and courage cannot be ascribed to the air, food, or the peculiar quality of the soil, but rather to good laws and discipline. The objections which have been raised against my assertion are of no significance. I readily admit that air and food can make for strong and sturdy beings, but from this it follows only that certain countries can, for physical reasons, beget strong and thriving poltroons.

The author of *L'Esprit des lois* accepts the general opinion in this matter, and since his judgments and considerations carry such weight, the number of persons who believe virtues and vices to be localized—that is, to be the natural effects of air, soil, and food—will become still greater. This same worthy and admirable writer confines himself to the subject in his seventeenth book, which begins with these words: "Great heat enervates human strength and courage. The cold climates give vigor to the body as well as the mind. This may be observed not only in comparing one nation with another but even the different parts of the same country. The northern inhabitants of China are more courageous than the southern; those in the northern part of Korea more so than those in the southern part." It is therefore no wonder, says he, that people in the warmer climates are slaves and acquiesce in despotic government, whereas they who live in cold countries will not submit to such. This all may be ascribed to natural conditions. Furthermore, he says that America serves as proof. The despotic or unlimited monarchies of Mexico and Peru were to be found along the equator, whereas most free peoples live near the poles.

I shall not cite what I previously have written about this and proved with so many examples from history that my point would seem irrefutable. I shall only examine the above-mentioned author's words briefly. It may readily be admitted that the cold countries give strength to the body, but it is not admissible that courage, virtue, and the desire for freedom come from the air and from food. One is born strong but is educated to courage and virtue. There is no sign of courage and bravery among the Samoyeds, Greenlanders, or other most northerly peoples. Before they were cultivated through laws and encouraged by good examples, the Russians were considered a cowardly and pacific people. Whether the northern inhabitants of America and Korea have more courage than the southern cannot be ascertained, for we have too little knowledge of these peoples. He says that the peoples in the warm countries are, so to speak, created to live in slavery and under absolutism. From this one would conclude that there can be found few or no examples of free republics in the southern part of the world, whereas history teaches us that the earliest Persian kings before the time of Cyrus ruled with less authority than the ancient northern princes and that they were looked upon more as *primi inter pares* or the leaders of the people than as monarchs. The same can be said about the ancient Egyptian kings, whom their subjects loved as children love their parents. Both countries were governed by profound, sensible, and moderate laws which cannot be read without evoking admiration. The objections which the author raises against the Chinese government cannot refute the reports of missionaries. At the arrival of the Spaniards in America, the republic of Tlaxcala was so great and mighty that it could hold its own against the Mexican monarchs. Midian, a large country in Asia, was long governed as a republic. In Palestine, or the land of the Philistines, the government was aristocratic. The Tyrians and the Phoenicians were formerly republicans. Carthage, which so long competed with Rome for the mastery of the world, was an African republic. There the heat of the sun had quite a different effect; no people has shown greater desire for freedom and independence than the Carthaginian. Lycia, a large country in Asia, consisted of twenty-three free states and was looked upon as a model for a republic of such size. The Greek states which border on Asia and which are not oppressed by cold viewed freedom as the most precious human possession, and it must be said that no cold and northerly country ever has loved independence more. Bosman, Artus, Barbot, and other travelers speak of aristocracies on the Gold Coast of Africa and of petty kings who have no authority governing in such places. As proof I could list other examples, but this suffices to make clear that significant criticism may be made of our author's conclusion.

There is no more forceful refutation of his conclusion than that of the changes to which the nations in question have been subjected. From this it follows that virtue and bravery, like learning, culture, and polite behavior, passed from one country to the other and indeed that every country has its ebb and flow. A bad ruler can make an entire country incompetent; a wise government is like Medea's cure, which can make dry twigs into blossoming branches. The Persians have alternately been belligerent, cowardly, and now belligerent again. Virtue, manliness, and knowledge seemed formerly to be concentrated in Greece. Now the old qualities have been transmuted into ignorance and cowardice. About Rome one can now say only, *hic seges ubi Troja fuit.* During the previous century the Russians were as docile as sheep; now they fight like lions. I shall not cite further examples in order not to repeat what I have written elsewhere. There is sufficient evidence to conclude what an insignificant role the heat of the sun and the northern cold play.

NOTES

EPISTLE 5

This Epistle, like Epistles 258 and 268, was occasioned by a German pamphlet entitled *Beweiss, dass die Universal-Monarchie vor die Wohlfahrt von Europa und überhaupt des menschlichen Geschlechts die gröste Glückseligkeit würcken würde,* Frankfurt and Leipzig, 1747.

tithings. Property on which tithings were paid to the University and which could be taken over and subleased by members of the University consistory. From 1722, Holberg held three such pieces of property.

Genghis Khan, Tamerlane. The subjects of the first chapter of Holberg's *Helte-Historier,* I, 1739. Mohammed II, Soliman II, and Peter the Great (one of Holberg's favorite historical figures) were treated in the same work.

a comet. In several places in his later works, Holberg makes satirical references to the superstitions regarding the great comet observed from December, 1743, through January, 1744.

an alliance. Presumably this refers to the coalition of England under William III with Spain, the United Provinces, and the Holy Roman Empire, prior to the Grand Alliance.

grand vizier. Ibrahim Pasha, killed in 1730 by order of the Sultan after the defeat of the Turks by Shah Nadir.

EPISTLE 7

Collins, Anthony (1676-1729). Of his several works the most important was *A Discourse on Freethinking,* 1713, a summation of the philosophy of English Freethinkers. Holberg owned his *Discourse of the Grounds and Reasons of the Christian Religion,* 1724. Epistle 466 is about Collins. BJ

Tindal, Matthew (1653-1733). Holberg owned his *Christianity as Old as Creation,* 1720, which had elicited some 150 replies.

Wholston. Thomas Woolston (1669-1731). Holberg owned his *Discourse on Miracles* (originally published 1726-28), which had evoked a series of refutations.

Morgan, Thomas (died 1743). Known principally as the author of *The Moral Philosopher,* 1737 ff.

excipere Forum. "Make an exception."

Hosea. Hosea 3:1 and 1:2.

Epistle 11

Holberg also discussed Freemasonry in Epistle 417.

The first Masonic lodge was established in Copenhagen by the secretary of the Russian legation in 1743. By 1750 there were three, two of which were recognized by London. The third was Scottish Rite and was oriented toward Berlin. German was the language of all the lodges.

excommunication. Freemasons were excommunicated by Pope Clement XII in 1738.

Rosicrucian Order. Rosicrucian societies which were parallel to the Masonic movement were established in imitation of the order which the Protestant theologian Johann Valentin Andreä described in anonymous satirical writings published 1614-16. Present-day Rosicrucians have no connection with the earlier "Rosenkreuzer."

girl in the comedy. Dorothea speaks in this way in Holberg's *Melampe,* I, 7; and Lucretia speaks similarly in the three-act version of *Den Vægelsindede* ("The Weathercock"), I, 8.

Alcibiades. The incident is mentioned in Plutarch's biography of Alcibiades, but Holberg may well be quoting at second hand.

fulmen brutum. Heat lightning.

Epistle 21

Bernard de Mandeville (1670-1733) was born in the Netherlands, studied at Leyden, and practiced medicine in England. *The Fable of the Bees: or, Private Vices, Publick Benefits* was first published in 1714, but it had been preceded in 1705 by the satirical poem *The Grumbling Hive*. *The Fable of the Bees* aroused much controversy and was attacked by William Law, Archibald Campbell, Thomas Bluett, George Berkeley, and others. Holberg owned Mandeville's book in a French translation, published in 1740. Mandeville was mentioned in *Moralske Tanker,* and the comedy *Plutus* suggests Holberg's interest in refuting Mandeville. BJ

Essenes. An ancient monastic, communistic, and puritanical Jewish sect which Holberg discusses sympathetically in his history of the Jews. BJ

Gymnosophists. Ancient sect of ascetic, nudist Hindu philosophers, the forerunners of the modern Jains.

Epistle 32

Le Clerc, Jean (Johannes Clericus, 1657-1736) is looked upon as a forerunner of modern Biblical criticism. His commentaries were published in Amsterdam, 1693-1733. Le Clerc also edited the widely read *Bibliothèque universelle et historique, Bibliothèque choisie,* and *Bibliothèque ancienne et moderne.*

Avenares. Ibn Ezra, i.e., Abraham ben Meir Ibn-Ezra, 1092-1167, Spanish Jewish poet, philosopher, grammarian, and traveler, best known for his rationalistic Bible commentaries.

Maimonides. Moses ben Maimon, 1135-1204, Spanish Jewish physician and scholar, who practiced medicine in Cairo and attempted a scientific study of Rabbinical literature.

Grotius, Hugo (1583-1645). Dutch jurist, scholar, and diplomat, best known for his *Mare liberum,* 1609, and *De*

jure belle et pacis, 1625. An Arminian, he also wrote on theological questions. He was a religious liberal and a rationalist, and advocated tolerance for all believers but not for atheists.

On the truth of the Christian faith. De Veritate Religionis Christianae, 1627, originally published as a poem in Dutch *(Bewys van den waeren Godsdienst),* was the most popular of Grotius' works. It went through many editions and was translated into several languages. There are Danish translations from 1678 and 1747. Le Clerc edited a late edition (1709) to which he appended an original essay.

syncretists. Those who would reconcile the various Christian churches. Holberg alludes to men like Grotius who wanted to reconcile the Lutheran, Reformed, and Roman Catholic churches.

Epistle 34

Bayle, Pierre (1647-1706). Best known for his *Dictionaire historique et critique,* which was Holberg's most important source of inspiration and material for the Epistles. The extent of Holberg's dependence on Bayle has been established by Billeskov Jansen in *Holberg som Epigrammatiker og Essayist,* II, *Essayisten,* Copenhagen, 1939. Bayle, a native of France, lived in Rotterdam from 1681 until his death. The son of a Calvinist clergyman, he—at one time a convert to Catholicism—was an advocate of tolerance. He was a prolific and cyclopaedic writer and polemicist. The Dictionary was written after Bayle had been discharged from his position as professor of philosophy and history in Rotterdam in 1693. Bayle was the butt of attacks by many critics particularly because of his hypothesis that a society of atheists might conceivably exist harmoniously. He was looked upon by many as an atheist, but he never confessed atheism or denied the existence of a Deity. He tried to explain the paradox of evil coexistent with divine goodness (incidentally the subject of

Holberg's first Epistle). Leibniz's *Théodicée* (1710) was an answer to Bayle.

Bayle's Dictionary was first published in two folio volumes, 1695-97. There were three later editions during Holberg's lifetime. Holberg owned the third edition. BJ

Bayle first attracted international attention with his so-called "Lettre sur les Comètes," i.e., *Lettre à M. L. A. D. C. Docteur de Sorbonne. Où il est prouvé par plusiers raisons tirées de la Philosophie, & de la Theologie, que les Comètes ne sont point le présage d'aucun malheur* . . . Cologne, 1682. The later editions bore the title *Pensées diverses* . . . .

Manichaeic. Pertaining to the doctrines of Manichaeus or Mani, *c.* 215-275, Persian religious leader who synthesized Zoroastrianism and Christianity. He assumed the existence of a positive evil as well as a positive good substance (Dualism).

Skeptic. Here referring to the extreme skepticism of Pyrrho, *c.* 365-275 B.C.

Epistle 39

Holberg's Epistles directed to the "Political College," of which this was the first, were generally of a humorous or jocular nature. Here he writes as if he were trying to avoid criticism.

Abbé de St. Pierre. Charles-Irénée Castel, Abbé de Saint-Pierre, 1658-1743, was a project-maker par excellence, as his *Ouvrajes de Politique,* first published in sixteen volumes, 1729-41, bears witness. Holberg refers either to the original *Projet pour rendre la paix perpétuelle en Europe,* 1713-16, or to the condensation, published as volume I of the *Ouvrajes,* Rotterdam, 1729. Holberg mentions St. Pierre in several other Epistles as well as in *Moralske Tanker.*

point d'argent . . . "no money, no Swiss."

War of the Spanish Succession (1701-13).

Epistle 41

Holberg spent the summers of his later years in the country, where he owned two estates. He became involved in lawsuits pursuant to the administration of his property.

Henrik Gøde (died 1676), *Christian Cassube* (died 1693) were printers in Copenhagen. Gøde published a German newspaper.

quartan fever. Characterized by the occurrence of paroxysms of the first and fourth days.

Epistle 45

ne sutor ultra crepidas. "Do not go above the sandal," i.e., "[shoemaker], stick to your last." According to Pliny the Elder, *Naturalis historia,* Book XXXV, chap. 36, the Greek painter Apelles accepted the advice of a shoemaker regarding a sandal in a painting, but remarked, *"Ne supra crepidam sutor iudicaret"* when the shoemaker expanded his criticism.

Æneas Sylvius. Enea Sylvio de Piccolomini, 1405-64, humanist and prolific writer, who ascended the papal throne as Pius II in 1458.

Conimbra. Coimbra, university seat in Portugal.

Salamanca. University seat in Spain, known for its theologians in the seventeenth century.

Epistle 48

The anecdote about the Devil is also found in Holberg's comedy *Philosophus udi egen Indbildning,* I, 3.

shoemaker of Jerusalem. Ahasuerus, the Wandering Jew.

Spain. Holberg was never in Spain.

Netherlands. The Low Countries.

stulti locum mutant. "Fools change their residence."

Peder Paars. Hero of Holberg's mock-heroic poem by the same name, first published 1719-20.

Tranquebar. Port in India, a Danish possession from 1616 to 1845.

Epistle 60

vindication of the donkey. Encomium asini by Agrippa of Nettesheim, 1486-1535, in his *De incertitudine et vanitate scientiarum atque artium,* Cologne, 1527, a satire on the learning of the day. BJ

Seven Wise Men, c. 600 B.C., first mentioned by Plato in *Protagoras.*

Dr. Faust. Epistle 95 discusses the Danish chapbook about Faust. Holberg felt it should be suppressed.

subscription. It was Holberg who introduced into Denmark the system of prepaid subscriptions to an author's announced work. It soon grew to be an abuse.

Minos, Rhadamanthus. Sons of Zeus and Europa who later became judges in Hades.

Gottfried Arnold (1666-1714), pietistic author of *Unpartheyische Kirchen- und Ketzerhistorie,* 1699-1700, which attempted to judge heretics on the basis of their utterances alone.

horns. The traditional symbol of a cuckold.

crab's-eyes. A stony substance found in the head, stomach, and other parts of a particular species of crab. Called *cancrorum oculi* in contemporary pharmacopoeias and considered to be absorbent and drying, "but also discussive and good against the Stone."

Zeno of Elea c. 490-430 B.C. Holberg discusses Zeno's hypothesis in Epistle 40. His source of information was Bayle's Dictionary, article "Zenon." Aristotle refuted Zeno in *Physics,* VI, 9.

Erasmus Montanus. Rasmus Berg, the leading character in Holberg's comedy *Erasmus Montanus.*

Peer the Deacon. The ignorant deacon in *Erasmus Montanus.*

Pastor Niels. Synecdoche for clergyman. He does not appear in *Erasmus Montanus,* although he does in several other comedies.

papal college. Actually existing in Copenhagen around

1718. Holberg participated in some of its meetings. This facetious consistory was the subject of Epistle 139.

Cardinal Orsini. Pope Benedict XIII, 1724-30, was an Orsini.

Epistle 64

Moral Thoughts. Moralske Tanker, 1744. Two German translations, one by Christian Gottlob Mengel and the other by Elias Caspar Reichard, appeared the same year. In Epistle 477, Holberg calls Reichard's translation incomparably better than Mengel's.

Matthaeus, Antonius (1635-1710). The reference is to his *De nobilitate . . . ,* 1686, Book II, chap. 20, but has been borrowed from Le Clerc's *Bibliothèque universelle et historique,* 1686, pp. 94-5. BJ

Loon trekkende Raadsheer. "Wage-drawing syndic."

Epistle 66

Euclio. In *Aulularia,* II, 4, verses 302-5.

Jacob von Tyboe eller den stortalende Soldat, inspired by Plautus' *Miles gloriosus;* first played in 1725.

Thraso. The boastful soldier in Terence's *Eunuchus.*

peccant, quia nihil peccant. "They err only in not erring." Adopted from Pliny the Younger, *Epistles,* 9, 26. BJ

Ulysses von Ithacia. A parody of the contemporary German tragedy; first played in 1724.

Henrik og Pernille. A comedy of servants' intrigue; first played in 1724.

Lamotte, Antoine Houdar de (1672-1731). Poet and modernist critic. His *Réflexions sur la critique* were published at The Hague in 1715.

Epistle 71

George Berkeley recommended tar water in his *Siris . . . ,* 1744. The original title was *Philosophical Reflexions and In-*

quiries Concerning the Virtues of Tar-Water. . . . The second edition was entitled *A Chain of Philosophical Reflexions,* and the third edition finally bore the title *Siris.* There were six editions in the first year of publication. The book was translated in whole or in part, into French, German, Dutch, Portuguese, and Spanish. It was reviewed in the *Bibliothèque Britannique,* XXIV, 1, 1746, pp. 83-98. Holberg may have read of the book there. Berkeley was the author of several lesser tracts on tar water. In *A Letter to T*[*homas*] *P*[*rior*], *Esq.* he wrote, "I freely own that I suspect tar-water is a panacea." Tar water, which was prepared by mixing tar and water and then draining off the water, was employed internally and externally for "fevers and pleurisies . . . itch, scabs, ulcers, leprosy . . . small-pox . . . gangrene in the blood." Berkeley felt it also to be beneficial in cases of drowsiness, itching eyes, deafness, idiocy, and cancer.

Holberg mentioned tar water several times. In Epistle 399, published in 1750, he noted that "tar water is no longer effective."

meat skewers. Danish, *Pølsepinde,* i.e., sausage pegs.

Epistle 72

Holberg's *Dannemarks og Norges Beskrivelse* was published in 1729. Second ed., 1749.

Spectators. Addison and Steele's *Spectator,* which succeeded *The Tatler,* first appeared in 1711 and was soon imitated all over Europe, and above all in Germany. *Spectator* literature did not really become popular in Denmark until after Holberg had published his *Moralske Tanker,* fundamentally a work of the same genre. The first Danish periodical employing the title *Spectator* appeared in 1738. A translation of the English *Spectator* was published 1742-43. In 1744-45, Jørgen Riis published *Den Danske Spectator* and a versified *Anti-Spectator* as well. Riis also wrote the *Politisk Tilskuer* in 1745. *Den Danske Spectators Philosophiske Spectator,* by Andreas Lundhoff, appeared from November, 1744, through January, 1745. The German dramatist J. E. Schlegel published *Der Fremde* in Copenhagen in 1745-46. Laurent Angliviel de La Beaumelle wrote *La Spectatrice Danoise, ou l'Aspasie moderne,* which was published in Copenhagen 1748-50. Many Danish periodicals of the *Spectator* type were published in the second half of the eighteenth century .

comet. The comet observed from December, 1743, through January, 1744, was one of the brightest ever recorded.

da capo. "[Repeat] from the beginning." *verte subito.* "Turn over quickly." Musical terms.

semper eadem. "Unchanging."

Epistle 79

Niels Klim was published in Latin in 1741 and was first translated into Danish the next year. It was translated into German, Dutch, and French in 1741, and into English in 1742. There are three English translations: (1) *A Journey to the World Under-Ground. By Nicholas Klimius . . .* , London, 1742. The translator is unknown. Title-editions appeared in 1746, 1749, and 1755. Reprinted in Edinburgh in 1812. (2) *Journey to the World under Ground; Being the Subterraneous Travels of Niels Klim* . . . London, 1828. (3) *Niels Klim's Journey under the Ground* . . . Translated from the Danish by John Gierlow . . . Boston and New York, 1845.

Quislimiri. Not mentioned in *Niels Klim.* This extension of the story was not included in the third edition.

Epistle 89

Holberg took the story of Hipparchia and Crates from Bayle's Dictionary, article "Hipparchia." BJ

a noble lady. Marie Grubbe (died 1718). She served as the model for Jens Peter Jacobsen's *Marie Grubbe* and also for one of the leading characters in Steen Steensen Blicher's *En Landsbydegns Dagbog.* From 1660 to 1670 she was the wife of Ulrik Frederik Gyldenløve, natural son of King Frederik III, and viceroy of Norway. Both her first and second husbands divorced her because of adultery. Her third husband, who had been employed as a coachman by her second husband, ran a ferry and lived on the island of Falster from 1706. It was there that Holberg met Marie Grubbe during an epidemic in Copenhagen.

Epistle 91

Holberg's principal source for this Epistle was Chambers' *Cyclopaedia,* articles "Coffee" and "Tobacco." In discussing tobacco, Chambers refers to the Grand Prior, Catherine de Medici, Jean Nicot, James I, Pope Urban VIII, and the word *petun.* BJ

vapors. Formerly believed to be produced within the body, to be harmful to the health, and to cause hypochondria.

Goldwasser. Danzig cordial.

Paulli, Simon (1603-80). Professor of Medicine at the University of Copenhagen. His *Commentarius de abusu tabaci Americanorum,* 1665, was published in English translation in 1746. Chambers mentions him.

Olearius, Adam (1604-71). Traveler and scholar. Author of *Offt Begehrte Beschreibung der Newen Orientalischen Reise,* 1647. There were several later editions. An English translation appeared in 1666.

Mandelslo, Johann Albrecht (1616-44). Traveled in Russia, India, Persia, and Africa. His journal was published in 1648.

De tribus impostoribus . . . . Holberg refers to a dissertation by Georg Detharding (1671-1747), published in Rostock in 1731.

Nicot, Jean (1530-1600). French ambassador to Portugal, who introduced tobacco into France.

Shah Abbas. Reigned 1586-1628. In his *Helte-Historier,* Holberg relates that Abbas gave dried horse manure to his guests, who thought it tobacco.

petun. Native South American name for tobacco.

Danish . . . poem. Tobacks Berømmelse, by Niels Lucoppidan, 1714.

Epistle 92

ghosts. Epistle 379 treats ghosts in much the same way as witchcraft is treated here. Holberg's comedy *Hexerie eller blind Alarm* ridiculed popular credulity.

Blocksberg or Hecla. According to popular superstition, witches assemble on these mountains, in Germany and Iceland respectively.

Loos, Cornelius (1546-95). Wrote *De vera et falsa magia* against witch hunts and witchcraft trials, but the book was suppressed.

Bekker, Balthasar (1634-98). Reformed clergyman, author of *De betoverde Weereld,* 1691-93, an attack on every sort of superstition. The book was widely read and aroused much controversy. Bekker subsequently lost his pastorate.

Finnmark. Lapland. The ecstatic delirium mentioned here is frequently referred to in literature about the Lapps.

Lork. Erich Lorch, *c.* 1647-1717, governmental representative in Lapland from 1701.

praestere praestanda. "Fulfill the obligation," "deliver the goods."

Neither Head nor Tail. Uden Hoved og Hale.

Epistle 99

Backgammon. Holberg writes "Back Game."

trick-track. Similar to backgammon. Danish, *Forkeering.*

le jeu d'echecs . . . . "The game of chess is not much of a game."

Epistle 109

Frederik IV (1671-1730). Traveled in Italy as crown prince, 1692-93, and as king, 1708-9.

courtier. Holberg may be referring to the king's favorite, Frederik Walter, 1649-1718. BJ

Chardin, Jean (1643-1713). Anglo-French traveler and scholar. His *Journal du voyage du chevalier Chardin en Perse et aux Indes Orientales,* London, 1686, was reprinted several times with varying title.

Dieu vous bénisse. "God bless you."

Epistle 112

third Latin epistle. Part three of Holberg's autobiography. The style of Holberg's *Opusculorum latinorum, pars Altera,* 1743, was censured in *Neuer Zeitungen von Gelehrten Sachen,* 1744, pp. 19 f.

Huetius. Pierre-Daniel Huet, 1630-1721, Prolific Jesuit scholar and polymath. Holberg's allusion is borrowed from Le Gendre, *Traité historique et critique de l'Opinion,* I, 1741, pp. 122 f.

Caligula, Gaius Caesar. Roman emperor A.D. 37-41. Suetonius' *Caligula* XXXIV, refers to the third book of Plato's *Republic.* From Le Gendre, I, 64.

Alcibiades. Ruthless Athenian politician and military leader of the fifth century B.C. From Le Gendre, I, 191, who has it from Plutarch. Since the anecdote is not found in the second edition of Le Gendre, it is evident that Holberg was using the third, of 1741.

Cato, Cicero, Scaliger. Le Gendre, I, 118-20.

Malherbe, François de (1555-1628). French poet and critic. From Le Gendre, I, 118 f.

Les ouvrages. . . . "Ordinary works live for a few years. That which Malherbe writes lasts forever."

Arrianus (c. 96-180). Greek philosopher and historian, author of the most important documentary history of Alexander the Great. Le Gendre, I, 119.

Epistle 121

Holberg's inspiration for this Epistle was Le Gendre's *Traité historique et critique de l'Opinion,* II, 270 ff. The allusions to Diodorus of Sicily, Egypt, and Anaximander are from Le Gendre.

Anaximander (611-547 B.C.) taught that all beings were formed from a mass of indestructible matter and that man must have sprung from a more primitive animal.

Metamorphosis. Metamorphosis eller Forvandlinger (1726), second ed., 1746.

Theogony. Often attributed to the early Greek poet Hesiod. It attempted a genealogy of the gods and a systematic enumeration of the various legends about them.

Merry-Andrew's opinion. The opinion of Henrich, the comic servant in Holberg's *Den Vægelsindede* ("The Weathercock"), five-act version, I, 2; three-act version, I, 6: "Now it may have happened that at the same time as my mistress was born a fox, a goose, a squirrel, an old cat, a deer, a tortoise, a fish, a magpie, a wolf, a lamb had died, and their souls had all gone to live in Madame's, where they still are and will be, as long as she is so changeable. Now when the goose's soul has control, she has the mind of a goose; when the wolf's soul gets the upper hand, I get beaten and spoken to roughly for nothing; and when the fish's soul is in power, she sits moping in company; and when the magpie's soul is in command, her mouth goes like the wheels of a mailcoach." (Translation by Henry Alexander, in *Four Plays by Holberg,* New York, 1946, p. 108.)

Epistle 130

Moral Thoughts. Holberg's *Moralske Tanker,* 1744.

Pufendorf, Samuel (1632-94). German historian and jurist on whose *De jure naturae et gentium,* 1672, Holberg based his *Introduction til Natur- og Folkeretten,* 1716.

Buddeus. Johann Franz Budde, 1667-1729, German theologian who taught at the universities of Wittenberg, Halle, and Jena. He was a friend of A. H. Francke and his theology was pietistically colored. His *Institutiones theologiae moralis variis observationibus illustratae,* was first published in Leipzig in 1711.

St. Jerome . . . whipped. Jerome himself relates the supposed scourging by divine command in *Epistola* XXII, 30.

The allusions and quotations from Seneca, Plato, Epictetus, Diogenes, and Epaminondas are borrowed from Le Gendre, *Traité historique et critique de l'Opinion,* III, Paris, 1741, pp. 161-83, 379.

Epictetus. The long quotation is from the *Discourses,* Bk. III, chap. 5.

Zaleukos, or Zaleucus (seventh century B.C.). The earliest Graeco-Roman lawgiver. The introduction to his legislation is cited by Diodorus of Sicily, Bk. XII, 20.

Epistle 135

Robeck, Johan (1672-1735). A native of Sweden. Converted to Catholicism in Germany; active as a Jesuit, 1705-34. His *Exercitatio philosophica . . .* was edited, with a foreword by Funccius and published at Rinteln, Prussia, in 1736.

Funccius. Johannes Nicolaus Funck, 1693-1777, prolific German writer and pedagogue.

Lactantius, Lucius Caecilius (*c.* 300). Early Christian apologist; criticized the approval of suicide by the Pythagoreans and Stoics in his *De divinis institutionibus,* III, 18.

Augustine. In *De civitate Dei,* I, 20, St. Augustine states that Christians have no authority for committing suicide under any circumstances whatsoever. He was the first to make suicide doctrinally a sin and a crime.

Epistle 141

ship . . . in the moon. A Danish soldier claimed to have seen a ship in the moon on February 13, 1713. His report and a sketch of the phenomenon are printed in *Danske sam-*

linger . . . , IV, 1868-69, pp. 363 ff. Holberg ridicules the tale in *Peder Paars,* I, 4, and in his comedy *Barselstuen,* II, 8. BJ

Montaigne. The passage is from the *Essais,* III, 11, but has been taken from Le Gendre, *Traité de l'Opinion,* V, 1741, p. 541.

Democritus. The anecdote, originally told by Plutarch about gherkins, not figs, is from Montaigne, II, 12, via Le Gendre, V, 541 f.

in Spain. From Le Gendre, V, 543 f.

Zahoris. Le Gendre has the word from Benito Geronimo Feyjoo in the latter's *Theatro critico universal, ó discursos varios,* Madrid, 1724-34. BJ

Plutarch. Le Gendre, V, 548, who has it from the so-called *Logique de Port Royal* of Antoine Arnauld and Pierre Nicole, first published in Paris in 1662. BJ

Epistle 157

The apology for the Devil was published in the same volume as Epistle 157 and had of course not "fallen into" anyone's hands.

Dr. Swift. The reference is to *A Complete Collection of Genteel and Ingenious Conversations, According to the Most Polite Mode and Method, Now used at Court, and in the Best Companies of England. In three Dialogues. By Simon Wagstaff, Esq.,* London, 1738. Holberg had apparently read only a review of the book, in the *Bibliothèque Britannique,* 1738, XI, 129 ff., for he misinterprets the book.

Some Thoughts concerning Happiness. By Irenæus Krantzovius [i.e., Benjamin Stillingfleet]. *Translated from the original German by A.B. with Notes.* London, 1738. The book, which was of course not a translation, was reviewed in *Bibliothèque Britannique,* 1739, XII, 70-81, but Billeskov Jansen points out that Holberg depended almost word for word on a review of a French translation of the work which, with another author's *A Letter to a Member of Parliament,* was published as *Traité Mathématique sur le Bonheur* in London in

1741. The review appeared in the same periodical, 1742, XVIII, 330-43. A German translation of a French translation was printed in 1745.

Volenti non . . . . "There is no offence to him who is willing to accept the offence." Quotation from *Bibliothèque Britannique.*

defense of the Devil. Cf. Epistle 60.

Epistle 158

Holberg is also satirizing the pietists in this Epistle.

Pliny. In a letter to Calvisius Rufus, Pliny cites the example of Spurinna, who followed an ordered and quiet life and who was well-preserved at the age of seventy-eight. *Epistles* of Pliny the Younger, III, 1.

Revelation's Master Key. Den aandelige Hovet-Nøgle til Himmelen, by Daniel Simon Paulli. First published in Copenhagen in 1680.

A True Christian's Nightcap. Holberg writes *En sand Christens Nat-Hue.* There is no book by this title.

Virtus eius incaluit mero . . . . Horace, Odes, 3, 21: "Narratur et prisci Catonis Saepe mero caluisse virtus." "It is said that even old Cato's virtue was heightened by wine."

Epistle 162

Theatrum Europæum. Theatrum Europæum, Oder Aussführliche und Warhafftige Beschreibung aller und jeder denckwürdiger Geschichten . . . 1617, biss auff das Jahr 1629 . . . Frankfurt, 1635 ff. 21 vols.

Mercuries. Holberg alludes to such publications as *Mercure de France,* of which several hundred volumes had been published by 1748, and *Mercure historique et politique contenant l'état présent de l'Europe.*

Epistle 189

filthy streets. The hygienic conditions of the streets in

Holberg's time left much to be desired. There were repeated complaints about street conditions and particularly about the unsatisfactory means of disposal of animal and human waste. Holberg mentions filthy streets in *Ulysses von Ithacia, Republiquen,* and other comedies.

Christianhavn's bridge. The present Knippelsbro across the so-called Inner Harbor. It connects Christianshavn with Copenhagen proper.

Epistle 190

Plautus and Molière were Holberg's masters in the writing of comedy. Holberg frequently contrasted Plautus and Terence, to the latter's disadvantage, as in Epistle 195. Holberg stressed the fact that Molière rewrote plays by Plautus but not by Terence. Holberg based three of his plays on comedies by Plautus: *Diderich Menschenschræk* on *Pseudolus, Jacob von Thyboe* on *Miles gloriosus,* and *Abracadabra* on *Mostellaria.*

Destouches. Philippe Néricault, called Destouches, 1680-1754, French diplomat and dramatist, was almost an exact contemporary of Holberg. His first comedy was played in 1709. His later comedies were not well received in France. Destouches is Holberg's whipping boy; he attacks him in several Epistles, notably 190, 493, and 511. Holberg adversely criticized the modern French drama in Epistles 296, 359, 360, 373, 374, 442, 447, and 506.

Terence. Holberg discussed Terence in the third part of his autobiography as well as in Epistle 195.

Epistle 211

Syllaba longa . . . . "A long syllable following a short is called iambic." Horace, *Ars poetica,* verse 251.

Christina (1626-89; queen, 1632-54). She corresponded with many learned men and called Descartes to Stockholm.

Bourdelot, Pierre Michon (1610-85). French physician

who spent some time at the Swedish court as the Queen's physician, 1652-53.

Meibom, Marcus (1626-1711). Published *Antiquae musicae auctores septem . . .* Amsterdam, 1652. Meibom left Stockholm for Denmark after the incident which Holberg mentions. Meibom was librarian of the Royal Library in Copenhagen until 1663.

Naudeaus. Gabriel Naudé (1600-1653). After Cardinal Mazarin's fall he was appointed librarian to Queen Christina of Sweden in 1652.

Epistle 232

De mundo optimo. "Of the best world," i.e., the best of all possible worlds, the conclusion of Leibniz's philosophical optimism in his *Essais de théodicée sur la bonté de Dieu, la liberté de l'homme et l'origine du mal,* Amsterdam, 1710 (and many later editions). No question aroused more discussion and theological controversy in the eighteenth century. The phrase cited here has been taken out of context and used promiscuously by many without any understanding of Leibniz's reasoning. It is of interest to note that, in 1741-45, the pietist Jeremias Friedrich Reuss published in Copenhagen a refutation of Leibniz's theodicy: *Doctrinae de mundo optimo brevis dilucidatio,* I-IV.

Wolf(f), Christian (1679-1754). Leibniz's disciple and the systematic philosopher of Rationalism. Wolf was the best-known philosopher of the early eighteenth century.

Naturalists. A general term for freethinkers and the believers in "natural," as opposed to revealed, religion.

Epistle 240

Holberg's own library was of a practical nature. It comprised many reference books but no choice bindings. Holberg willed his library to the academy at Sorø, where it burned in 1813. Christian Bruun reconstructed a part of Holberg's library: *Fortegnelse over en Del af Ludvig Holbergs Bibliothek,* 1869.

rubrics. Titles of laws. Originally so called because printed in red, just as many title-pages formerly were.

Hercules Herculiscus. Holberg alludes to two books by Andreas Heinrich Buchholz (1607-71), one of the first Germans to write in the gallant style of the seventeenth century novel: *Des Christlichen Teutschen Gross-Fürsten Herkules . . . ,* 1659-60, and *Des Christlichen Teutschen Gross-Fürsten Herkuliskus . . . ,* 1665. Holberg made the same allusion in *Den politiske Kandestøber,* I, 4.

Astrea. L'Astrée by Honoré d'Urfé (1568-1625); originally published in five volumes, 1607-19, 1627. It was completed after D'Urfé's death by his secretary. In the Amadis tradition, *L'Astrée* was the most exemplary of the gallant novels of the century. It was partly translated into Danish from the German version, 1645-48. Holberg also mentions the book in *Den Vægelsindede,* II, 12.

Dr. Faust. A Danish translation of the German *Historia von D. Johann Fausten,* 1587, was published in 1588, but no perfect copy of this translation is extant. It was reprinted in Lund in 1674, 1685, and 1698. The German "Christlich Meynender" Faust-book was translated into Danish in 1732.

Danish plays. Holberg's own plays.

Dr. Spener. Philip Jacob Spener, 1635-1705, the founder of German pietism. His best-known work was *Pia desideria . . . ,* 1675.

Epistle 241

She hates him worse than a Quaker . . . . Spoken by Witwoud at the end of Act I in Congreve's *The Way of the World.*

Sputt'ring at one another . . . Spoken by Witwoud after his entrance in Act IV. Holberg quotes in English.

Epistle 254

Epistle 214 is on Chinese plays, 246 on Chinese agriculture, 251 on the Chinese language, and 253 on religious conditions in China. Holberg's chief source of information was the compendious *Description géographique, historique, chronologique, politique, et physique de L'Empire de la Chine et de la Tartarie chinoise* by the French Jesuit Jean-Baptiste Du Halde (1674-1743). The work was first published in 1735, in four folio volumes. English translation, 1736; German translation, 1747-49. Du Halde was never in China but drew on the memoirs of a number of missionaries.

Ricci, Matteo (1552-1610). Italian Jesuit missionary. The reference is probably to *De Christiana expeditione apud Sinas,* 1615, but is taken from Du Halde, III, 274.

Lecomte, Louis *(c.* 1656-1729). Jesuit missionary. Wrote *Nouveaux Mémoires sur l'état present de la Chine,* I-II, 1696. Du Halde, III, 275 ff.

Dentrecolles, François-Xavier (1662-1741). Jesuit missionary.

novels. After Du Halde, III, 292 ff. Holberg relates Du Halde's *"Autre Histoire,"* III, 324 ff.

Epistle 260

The Craftsman. By Caleb D'Anvers, of Gray's Inn, Esq., London, 1726-36. The editor was Nicholas Amhurst (1697-1742). Viscount Bolingbroke and William Pulteney, Earl of Bath, were contributors. It was the most widely read of contemporary British political journals.

Old England: or, The Constitutional Journal, London, 1743-51. Edited by William Guthrie (1708-70). Horace Walpole was a contributor. The argument which Holberg cites is not found in the issues of the periodical preserved in the Yale University Library (January, 1743, to April, 1748), but the issue of May 25, 1745, states that the Netherlands would be "content for the sake of Peace, to sit down with a less *Barrier,* than their own immediate Safety required." The editorial in the issue of August 23, 1746, expresses the same view as Holberg.

Duchess of Marlborough. Sarah Jennings Churchill (1660-1744) left £10,000 to William Pitt.

Pitt. Holberg's text has "Witte."

EPISTLE 335

republic . . . of atheists. The country Mikolac in Holberg's *Niels Klim,* chap. 8.

one of M. Bayle's paradoxes. The reference is to article "Epicure," note D, in Bayle's Dictionary. Holberg discussed the question again in Epistle 477.

Cicero. De finibus bonorum et malorum, I, chap. 20. Quoted by Bayle. BJ

Diocles of Karystos (fourth century B.C.). The incident is described in article "Epicure," note N.

EPISTLE 342

Herodian. Third century Greek historian. His history covers the years 180-238.

Comineus. Philippe de Comines, Sieur d'Argenton, 1445 1509. His memoirs are a chronicle of the times of Louis XI and Charles VIII.

French overture. Followed the model set by Lully in the operatic overture to his ballet *Alcidiane,* 1658. The "French overture" was popular until about 1750.

EPISTLE 390

testimonial. In Holberg's *Niels Klim,* chap. 4. It reads: "Whereas the learned and venerable Jocthan Hu has required of his neighbors a testimonial of his life and morals, we the citizens living in that street or portion of the city called Posko, do testify, that the said Jocthan Hu has lived in wedlock for four full years with a disloyal wife, and that without the least noise or disturbance; that he has worn his horns with a laudable patience, and with such meekness has born this misfortune, that we judge him highly worthy to succeed the vacant mastership, if his learning be equal to his morals. Given under our hands this 10th day of the month Palm, in the 3000ndth year after the great deluge." (After *A Journey to the World Under-Ground,* London, 1742, pp. 56 f.)

Epistle 395

Holberg's own works were subject to censorship. Censorship was not actually abolished in Denmark until 1849.

Let them stay in Jericho. I Chronicles 19:5 and II Samuel 10:5.

subterranean ordinance. In the state of Potu, in Holberg's *Niels Klim,* chap. 8, none might write books before the age of thirty and before having been declared capable by the academic authorities.

Epistle 400

Holberg wrote about Queen Elizabeth in his *Introduction . . . ,* 1711, as well as in *Heltinde-Historier,* 1745. His source was Rapin Thoyras, *Histoire d'Angleterre,* 1724, VI, 145 ff. BJ

Höchstädt. Marlborough defeated the French and Bavarians at Blenheim near Höchstädt August 13, 1704.

Ramillies. Marlborough defeated the French there May 23, 1706.

Epistle 433

Childrey, Joshua (1623-70). English clergyman, antiquary, and astrologer. Author of *Britannica Baconica; or, The Natural Rarities of England, Scotland & Wales . . .* London, 1661. The book also appeared in French. Childrey believed that he was combating superstition. On p. 22 he wrote, "Some Gentlemen in this Country have for their delight Salt-water pond, into which if you cast boughes of trees, Oysters will grow upon them."

Epistle 441

The Bewitched Bowl. La Coupe enchantée by Jean de La Fontaine (1621-95), author of the *Fables,* and Charles Chevillet de Champmeslé (died 1701). First played 1688. Published 1710 under the name of Chammelay. Danish translation published 1748.

Vulcan's Rod. La Baguette de Vulcain by Jean François Regnard (1655-1709), and Charles Dufresny, Sieur de la Rivière (1648-1724). This short comedy in six scenes had its debut in 1693. First played in Denmark and published in Danish translation in 1748.

The Oracle. L'Oracle, Comedie en un acte et en prose by Germain-François Poullain de Saint-Foix (1698-1776). First played in 1740; published anonymously. First played in Denmark in 1748; translation published the same year.

Aspasie. La Spectatrice Danoise, ou l'Aspasie moderne, a periodical written by Laurent Angliviel de la Beaumelle (1726-73) and published in Copenhagen 1748-50. The disparaging remark to which Holberg refers was contained in "Amusement XLV."

Corelli, Arcangelo (1653-1713). Italian violinist and composer, the creator of the *concerto grosso.*

Jean de France. One of Holberg's earliest and most successful plays, first given in 1722.

Epistle 452

The idea in this arresting Epistle was not original with Holberg. Billeskov Jansen points out that it was taken from an imaginary conversation included in Noël-Antoine Pluche's *Le Spectacle de la Nature,* I, 288-92. Pluche's work, first published anonymously in 1732, was of popular nature. Although he utilized it in writing several Epistles, Holberg mentioned Pluche only once, in Epistle 454.

alchemy. An allusion to Epistle 117.

Epistle 467

L'Homme Machine. By Julien Offray de La Mettrie (1709-51). Published anonymously in Leyden in 1748. It contained a long and satirical dedication to the Swiss poet and physician Albrecht von Haller. The book evoked numerous refutations, but none from famous pens other than Haller's. An English translation of La Mettrie's book appeared in 1749.

La Mettrie, a French physician and philosopher, fled to Holland after his earlier work, *Histoire naturelle d'ame,* had been publicly burned after its publication at The Hague in 1745. He was soon called to Berlin by Frederick the Great. La Mettrie, who later wrote several other works of materialistic philosophy, is looked upon as a forerunner of modern philosophical materialism and comparative biology.

Epistle 483

allez. Literally, "go!"

vous vous moquez de moi. "You are making fun of me," i.e., "You don't mean it."

On le garde pour vous. "They are keeping it for you." Billeskov Jansen thinks Holberg misunderstood the bookdealer's sentence.

Holberg criticized other Parisian foibles, especially the predilection for fine attire, in his autobiography. He was nevertheless fond of Paris and resided there for several months in 1714-15 and 1725-26.

Epistle 506a

Riccoboni, Luigi (1674-1753). Called Lelio. Italian theatrical director who established himself in Paris at the Hôtel de Bourgogne. He wrote several critical works, of which the most important is the *Histoire du Théâtre Italien,* Paris, 1728-31. Holberg's source for this Epistle was Riccoboni's *Observations sur la Comédie, et sur le Génie de Molière,* 1736, 143 ff.

L'inavertito. By Nicolò Barbieri, called Beltrame. Printed 1630.

L'Amoroso sdegno. By Francesco Bracciolini. Printed 1597.

Arlichino Medico non Volento. Refers to the scenario *Arlecchino Medico Volante* by Domenico Biancolelli the Elder. A. Kugel, *Zschr. f. franz. Sprache u. Litteratur,* 1898, XX, 1-17, concludes that Molière's play was not derived directly from the Italian scenario.

Disgrazie d'Arlichino. Later critics have not substantiated this hypothesis. Cf. H. C. Lancaster, *A History of French Dramatic Literature in the Seventeenth Century,* 1936, Part III, vol. 2, pp. 718 ff.

Il Dottor Bachettone. There are several theories, none of them compelling, regarding Molière's source for *Tartuffe.* Holberg's (i.e., Riccoboni's) suggestion is not accepted by modern scholars.

L'École des maris and George Dandin. Riccoboni: "On trouve la Fable de *l'École des Maris* dans la troisiéme Nouvelle de la troisiéme Journée du Décameron du *Bocace;* celle de George-Dandin, dans deux autres Nouvelles du même Auteur, qui sont celle *d'Arriguccio Berlinghieri* . . . & celle de *Tofano* . . . ." There were probably several sources for *L'École des maris,* including Boccaccio and Terence.

Arlichino cornuto per opinione. Molière's *Sganarelle ou le Cocu imaginaire* resembles plays by Scarron and Boisrobert rather than the Italian commedia which Riccoboni and Holberg name. In his *Réflexions, historiques et critiques sur les différens théâtres de l'Europe,* Paris, 1738, Riccoboni himself says of *L'Étourdi, Dépit amoureux, Les Précieuses ridicules, Cocu imaginaire,* and *LÉcole des maris,* "Ces Pièces, qui ne ressembloient à rien de tout ce que l'on avoit vu dans les Anciens &

dans les Modernes . . . ." (Page 97 in the edition published in Amsterdam, 1740.)

Festin de Pierre. Don Juan, probably written after the model of plays by the earlier French dramatists Dorimon and Villiers. The ultimate source of the Don Juan play seems to be *El Burlador de Sevilla,* 1630, by Gabriel de Téllez, called Tirso de Molina.

The Miser. L'Avare and *Amphitryon* were based on Plautus' *Aulularia* and *Amphitryon.*

The Weathercock. Den Vægelsindede. Destouches' *L'Irrésolu* is older than Holberg's comedy. It was first played in 1713 and Holberg's comedy was written ten years later.

The Fussy Man. Den Stundesløse.

Plutus, Philosophus udi egen Indbildning, and *Republiquen eller Det gemeene Beste* were published posthumously in 1754.

Epistle 516

Holberg treats of Montesquieu's *L'Esprit des loix* in Epistles 514, 516, 517, 519, and 520. Epistles 111, 514, and 516-19 were separately published in French in 1753 as *Remarques sur . . . l'Esprit des loix.* Epistle 526b also discusses Montesquieu. *De l'Esprit des loix* was published anonymously in 1748.

Tlaxcala. Independent Mexican republic which was surrounded by the Aztec empire.

Midian. An area of northwestern Arabia.

Lycia. Area in southwest Asia Minor; in ancient times an independent country.

Bosman, William (born 1672). Employee of the Netherlands East Indies Co., wrote *Nauwkeurige Beschryving van de Guinese Goud-, Tand-, en Slave-Kust,* Utrecht, 1704, which was translated into French, German, English, and Latin. Billeskov Jansen believes that Holberg's acquaintance with Bosman, Arthus, and Barbot was at second hand.

Arthus, Gotthard (1570-*c.* 1630). Translated several books of travel from the Dutch. Holberg alludes to *Warhafftige*

Historische Beschreibung dess gewaltigen Goltreichen Königreichs Guinea, Frankfurt, 1603, published as part six of a series, *Des Orientalischen Indien,* which also appeared in Latin.

Barbot, Jean (died 1720). French traveler. His French manuscript was translated and published in London in 1732 as *A Description of the Coasts of North and South-Guinea* . . . which was the fifth volume of Churchill's *A Collection of Voyages and Travels.* The reference is to chapter 23 of Barbot's work.

Medea's cure. Medea possessed the power of rejuvenation. Ovid, *Metamorphoses* VII, 279 ff.

Hic seges ubi Troja fuit. Ovid, *Heroides* I, 53, "Iam seges est, ubi Troia fuit," "Now are fields of grain where Troy was."

INDEX

Index

www.ingramcontent.com/pod-product-compliance
Lightning Source LLC
Chambersburg PA
CBHW070820020826
48982CB00014B/105